BIBLE STUDY GUIDE

JESUS:
King or Concierge?

A STUDY OF THE
Gospel of Matthew

Brian Harbour
Ronnie & Renate Hood
Ronny Marriott
Julie Wood

BAPTISTWAYPRESS®
Dallas, Texas

Jesus: King or Concierge? A Study of the Gospel of Matthew—
Connect 360 Bible Study Guide

BAPTISTWAY PRESS® Leadership Team
Executive Director, Baptist General Convention of Texas: David Hardage
Director, Discipleship Team: Phil Miller
Publisher, BaptistWay Press®: Scott Stevens

Cover: Micah Kandros Design
Interior Design and Production: Desktop Miracles, Inc.
Printing: Data Reproductions Corporation

First edition: December 2015
ISBN–13: 978–1–938355–45–5

ALL THE BIBLE FOR ALL OF LIFE

Introducing Connect 360

Welcome to the first edition of Connect 360: All the Bible for All of Life from BaptistWay Press®. Connect 360 communicates our mission to connect people to God through his word. Our Bible study materials are designed to equip people everywhere to discover biblical truth, to believe the truth revealed in the Bible, and to live out this truth in their everyday lives. You see this represented in our new "Discover-Believe-Live" logo which outlines this discipleship process.

Discover. Believe. Live.
A discipleship strategy focused on discovering, believing, and living out the truths of the Bible.

All the Bible for All of Life
Connect 360 exists to show all of the Bible as instrumental in revealing God's purpose and plan for life.

As evidenced in our new tagline "All the Bible for All of Life," we believe God's word provides the wisdom and guidance we need to accomplish his will in the world. We also believe the Bible contains the truth we need to meet the challenges of life. We're excited to unveil this new look as we continue to provide trusted, biblical resources for you and your church.

Since 1999, BaptistWay Press® has published high quality Bible study resources, written by trusted Baptist authors. We commit to you to continue producing the same quality studies you expect from BaptistWay, written by Baptists who remain true to the biblical text and its interpretation. We believe all of the Bible, in its proper context, can teach and guide every part of our lives. Our mission is to help you and your church Discover the Truth of Scripture, Believe it, and Live it out every day. Welcome to Connect 360.

How to Make
the Best Use of This Issue

Whether you're the teacher or a student—

1. Start early in the week before your class meets.

2. Overview the study. Review the table of contents and read the study introduction. Try to see how each lesson relates to the overall study.

3. Use your Bible to read and consider prayerfully the Scripture passages for the lesson. (You'll see that each writer has chosen a favorite translation for the lessons in this issue. You're free to use the Bible translation you prefer and compare it with the translation chosen for that unit, of course.)

4. After reading all the Scripture passages in your Bible, then read the writer's comments. The comments are intended to be an aid to your study of the Bible.

5. Read the small articles—"sidebars"—in each lesson. They are intended to provide additional, enrichment information and inspiration and to encourage thought and application.

6. Try to answer for yourself the questions included in each lesson. They're intended to encourage further thought and application, and they can also be used in the class session itself.

If you're the teacher—

Do all of the things just mentioned, of course. As you begin the study with your class, be sure to find a way to help your class know the date on which each lesson will be studied. You might do this in one or more of the following ways:

A. In the first session of the study, briefly overview the study by identifying for your class the date on which each lesson will be studied. Lead your class to write the date in the table of contents on page 9 and on the first page of each lesson.

- Make and post a chart that indicates the date on which each lesson will be studied.
- If all of your class has e-mail, send them an e-mail with the dates the lessons will be studied.
- Provide a bookmark with the lesson dates. You may want to include information about your church and then use the bookmark as an outreach tool, too. A model for a bookmark can be downloaded from www.baptistwaypress.org on the **Adults—Bible Studies** page.
- Develop a sticker with the lesson dates, and place it on the table of contents or on the back cover.
- Get a copy of the *Teaching Guide*, a companion piece to this *Study Guide*. The *Teaching Guide* contains additional Bible comments plus two teaching plans. The teaching plans in the *Teaching Guide* are intended to provide practical, easy-to-use teaching suggestions that will work in your class.

B. After you've studied the Bible passage, the lesson comments, and other material, use the teaching suggestions in the *Teaching Guide* to help you develop your plan for leading your class in studying each lesson.

C. Teaching resource items for use as handouts are available free at www.baptistwaypress.org.

D. Additional Bible study comments on the lessons are available in digital format. Call 1–866–249–1799 or e-mail baptistway@texasbaptists.org to order the *Premium Bible Commentary*. It is available only in digital format (PDF) from our website, www.baptistwaypress.org. The price of these comments for the entire study is $5 per person. A church or class that participates in our advance order program for free shipping can receive the *Premium Bible Commentary* free. Call 1–866–249–1799 or see www.baptistwaypress.org to purchase or for information on participating in our free shipping program for the next study.

E. Additional teaching plans are also available in digital format (PDF) by calling 1–866–249–1799. The price of these additional teaching plans for the entire study is $5 per person. A church or class that participates in our advance order program for free shipping can receive the *Premium Teaching Plans* free. Call 1–866–249–1799 or see www.baptistwaypress.org for information on participating in our free shipping program for the next study.

F. You also may want to get the enrichment teaching help that is provided on the Internet by the *Baptist Standard* at www.baptiststandard.com. (Other class participants may find this information helpful, too.) The *Baptist Standard* is available online for an annual subscription rate of $10. Subscribe online at www.baptiststandard.com or call 214–630–4571. (A free thirty-day trial subscription is currently available.)

G. Enjoy leading your class in discovering the meaning of the Scripture passages and in applying these passages to their lives.

Do you use a Kindle?

This Connect 360 *Bible Study Guide* plus *Created for Relationships; 14 Habits of Highly Effective Disciples; Guidance for the Seasons of Life; Living Generously for Jesus' Sake; Profiles in Character; Exodus: Liberated for Life in Covenant with God; Psalms: Songs from the Heart of Faith; Amos, Hosea, Isaiah, Micah; Jeremiah and Ezekiel; The Gospel of Mark; The Gospel of Luke: Jesus' Personal Touch; The Gospel of John: Believe in Jesus and Live!; The Book of Romans: A Gospel-Centered Worldview; The Book of Acts: Time to Act on Acts 1:8; The Corinthian Letters: Imperatives for an Imperfect Church; Hebrews and the Letters of Peter;* and *Letters to the Ephesians and Timothy* are now available in a Kindle edition. The easiest way to find these materials is to search for "BaptistWay" on your Kindle or go to www.amazon.com/kindle and do a search for "BaptistWay." The Kindle edition can be studied not only on a Kindle but also on a PC, Mac, iPhone, iPad, Blackberry, or Android device using the Kindle app available free from amazon.com/kindle.

Writers for This *Study Guide*

Julie Wood wrote **lessons one through three**. She is a graduate of Hardin-Simmons University and Southwestern Baptist Theological Seminary. She loves ministering with her husband, Dr. Darin Wood, pastor of Central Baptist Church in Jacksonville, Texas; and being mother to their son, Joshua. A former children's minister and worship leader, she now serves as a free-lance writer and accompanist for Jacksonville Independent School District choirs and bands.

Ronny Marriott, the writer of **lessons four through seven**, is pastor of First Baptist Church, Temple, Texas. He holds the Doctor of Ministry degree from Southwestern Baptist Theological Seminary.

Brian Harbour wrote **lessons eight through ten**. Dr. Harbour has spent a lifetime teaching God's word and encouraging God's people. He served nine different churches in his forty-two years as a pastor of a local church. In his teaching ministry, he taught as a visiting professor or adjunct professor at Baylor University, George W. Truett Seminary, and Dallas Baptist University. In his writing ministry, he has authored seventeen books and for twenty-seven years produced a bi-monthly journal for pastors that included sermons, outlines, illustrations, and articles on preaching and leadership. He continues his ministry of encouragement through his non-profit organization, *SeminaryPLUS*.

Ronnie and Renate Hood wrote **lessons eleven through thirteen and the Christmas lesson**. Dr. Ronnie W. Hood II is senior pastor of Canyon Creek Baptist Church, Temple, Texas. He is a graduate of Samford University, Birmingham, Alabama. Dr. Renate Viveen Hood is professor of Christian Studies (New Testament and Greek) at the University of Mary Hardin-Baylor, Belton, Texas. She earned medical science degrees in the Netherlands. The

Hoods studied at New Orleans Baptist Theological Seminary, where Ronnie earned M.Div., Th.M., and Ph.D. (Church History) degrees, and Renate earned M.Div. and Ph.D. (Biblical Studies and Greek) degrees.

Jesus: King or Concierge?
A STUDY OF THE GOSPEL OF MATTHEW

DATE OF STUDY

UNIT ONE

The Advent of the King

UNIT TWO

The Manifesto of the King

Introducing

Jesus: King or Concierge?
A STUDY OF THE GOSPEL OF MATTHEW

Approaching This Study of the Gospel of Matthew

Are you familiar with the term "concierge?" It usually refers to an attendant or a caretaker (especially at a residence or hotel.) Perhaps you've enjoyed the services of a concierge when you have traveled. They can provide timely assistance in meeting the needs, wants, and desires of the guests under their care.

Unfortunately, people often treat Jesus as their personal concierge. They view him as someone who generally is not seen and is only wanted around when there is a problem to be solved or a need to be met. Other than those times, they would rather not be bothered by any demands Jesus might place on their lives. Some have referred to this practice as the "Jesus in my pocket syndrome," where Jesus is only pulled out of the pocket if a crisis arises. Others claim that such practice treats Jesus more as a mascot than a master.

The Gospel of Matthew declares that Jesus Christ is not a concierge but a King who deserves our loyalty and obedience. The royalty of Jesus is demonstrated from the beginning of the Gospel: from Jesus' lineage which proves him to be the Son of David, to the Magi who seek the King of the Jews, to the title of King that is mockingly added to the sign above the cross at his crucifixion.

Jesus is revealed as the King of kings because he was conceived of the Holy Spirit (1:18–25); received gifts and worship from the Magi (2:1–12); was

affirmed by his Father at his baptism (3:16–17); defeated Satan's temptations (4:1–11); taught with authority (7:28–29); demonstrated his power to
heal (8:1–13); and defeated death (28:1–10). All of these incidents and others
recorded in the Gospel of Matthew point to Jesus as King.[1]

Jesus preached and taught extensively about the kingdom of heaven. His
Sermon on the Mount (the Manifesto of the King) lays out the expectations
of kingdom citizens and interprets much of the Old Testament Law in light
of his coming. He also affirms his fulfillment of the Law and the prophets:

> Do not think that I have come to abolish the Law or the Prophets;
> I have not come to abolish them but to fulfill them. I tell you the
> truth, until heaven and earth disappear, not the smallest letter,
> not the least stroke of a pen, will by any means disappear from
> the Law until everything is accomplished. (Matthew 5:17–18).[2]

Matthew records parables that Jesus used to illustrate the nature of his
kingdom. In Jesus' explanation to his disciples about his choice of using parables he states:

> 'The knowledge of the secrets of the kingdom of heaven has been
> given to you, but not to them. Whoever has will be given more,
> and he will have an abundance. Whoever does not have, even
> what he has will be taken from him. This is why I speak to them
> in parables: 'Though seeing, they do not see; though hearing, they
> do not hear or understand' (Matt. 13:11–13).

Matthew also presents Jesus' reply as he is questioned by the high priest
at one of his trials,

> The high priest said to him, 'I charge you under oath by the living
> God: Tell us if you are the Christ, the Son of God.' 'Yes, it is as you
> say,' Jesus replied. 'But I say to all of you: In the future you will see
> the Son of Man sitting at the right hand of the Mighty One and
> coming on the clouds of heaven.' (Matt. 26:63b–64)

Those are the words of a king, not a caretaker!

Perhaps the most familiar words in Matthew's Gospel are what we know as the Great Commission:

> Then Jesus came to them and said, 'All authority in heaven and on earth has been given to me. Therefore go and make disciples of all nations, baptizing them in the name of the Father and of the Son and of the Holy Spirit, and teaching them to obey everything I have commanded you. And surely I am with you always, to the very end of the age.'

These final words of Jesus in the Gospel of Matthew are the King's marching orders for his church. They are based on his authority and are not presented as optional. We can also be confident of his presence with us as we carry out his command. The question then becomes, will his followers obey their king?

Since the beginning of our BaptistWay Bible study series, we have focused on the Book of Matthew four previous times (the last time was in 2011.)[3]

We think studying Scriptures directly about Jesus on a regular basis is important, so we provide a study of a Gospel each year. Each study begins with a new emphasis and fresh outlines and lessons are created.

Background Information on the Gospel of Matthew

The Gospel of Matthew was written by the former tax collector (Matthew), one of the original twelve apostles. The numerous Old Testament references found in the Gospel likely indicate it was written for a primarily Jewish audience. There is great care taken to show Jesus as the long-awaited Messiah who was described by the prophets in the Old Testament. Many scholars believe the Book of Matthew was written sometime between 60–70 A.D.

The term "Kingdom of heaven" that is used in Matthew is an exclusively Jewish phrase and only appears in this Gospel. Matthew also has much to say about the law, religious defilement, the Sabbath, Jerusalem, the temple, David, the Messiah, and Moses.[4]

The main themes of the Gospel of Matthew include:
- Jesus Christ the King
- The Messiah
- Kingdom of God
- Jesus' Teaching
- Resurrection and Commission[5]

The Gospel of Matthew in Our Day

How should the Gospel of Matthew impact Jesus' followers today? A study of Matthew gives us the opportunity to evaluate our beliefs and practice regarding Jesus. As Jim Denison has written, Is Christ your King, or is he a "hobby?" Jim has stated,

> If God is your King, you're breathing his air, wearing his clothes, walking on his planet. He's your King on Monday, not just Sunday. He's King of what you keep, not just what you give. He's King of what you do in private, not just what you do in public.
>
> For many people today, God is a hobby. Our society believes that Christianity is for church and religion is for Sunday. Our faith is to be kept separate from the 'real world.' Your neighbors don't mind if you go to church on Sunday morning, but don't tell them they have to go to church. Everyone "knows" that so long as you believe in God and live a good life you'll go to heaven. Less than one percent of Americans are afraid they might go to hell.[6]

Our prayer is that this study of the Gospel of Matthew will reawaken us all to the majesty of King Jesus. May the result of this awakening be fruitful lives actively involved in serving our King and completing his commission.

Additional Resources for Studying the Gospel of Matthew[7]

William Barclay. *The Gospel of Matthew.* The *New* Daily Study Bible. Louisville, KY: Westminster John Knox Press, 2001.

Kenneth L. Barker and John R. Kohlenberger III. *The Expositor's Bible Commentary—Abridged Edition: New Testament.* Grand Rapids, Michigan: Zondervan, 1994.

Bruce Barton, Philip Comfort, Grant Osborne, Linda K. Taylor, and Dave Veerman. *Life Application New Testament Commentary.* Carol Stream, Illinois: Tyndale House Publishers, Inc., 2001.

Craig L. Blomberg. "Matthew." *The New American Commentary.* Volume 22. Nashville: B&H Publishing Group, 1992.

M. Eugene Boring. "Matthew." *The New Interpreter's Bible*. Volume VIII. Nashville: Abingdon Press, 1995.

R.T. France. *The Gospel of Matthew*. The New International Commentary on the New Testament. Grand Rapids, Michigan: William B. Eerdmans Publishing Company, 2007.

David Garland. *Reading Matthew*. Macon, Georgia: Smyth and Helwys Publishing, Inc., 1999.

Craig S. Keener. *IVP Bible Background Commentary: New Testament*. Downers Grove, Illinois: InterVarsity Press, 1993.

A.T. Robertson. *Word Pictures in the New Testament: Concise Edition*. Nashville, Tennessee: Holman Bible Publishers, 2000.

Spiros Zodhiates and Warren Baker. *Hebrew-Greek Key Word Study Bible, New International Version*. Grand Rapids, Michigan: Zondervan, 1996.

Notes

1. Bruce Barton, Philip Comfort, Brant Osborne, Linda K. Taylor, and Dave Veerman. *Life Application New Testament Commentary* (Carol Stream, Illinois: Tyndale House Publishers, Inc., 2001), 7.

2. Unless otherwise indicated, all Scripture quotations in "Introducing Jesus: King or Concierge?" are from the New International Version (1984 edition).

3. See www.baptistwaypress.org.

4. Bruce Barton, Philip Comfort, Brant Osborne, Linda K. Taylor, and Dave Veerman, 4.

5. Ibid., 7.

6. http://lovegod.denisonforum.org/heart/383-have-you-made-christ-your-king. Accessed 1/23/15.

7. Listing a book does not imply full agreement by the writers or BAPTISTWAY PRESS® with all of its comments.

The Advent of the King

Unit One, "The Advent of the King" contains three lessons that tell the story of Jesus' miraculous birth, John the Baptist' role in announcing the coming of the Messiah, and the account of Jesus' temptation experience in the wilderness. Lesson one describes how Jesus' birth fulfilled prophecy and elicited worship. Lesson two reveals how John the Baptist's prophetic preaching prepared the way for Jesus, and how the unfolding events at Jesus' baptism confirmed his identity as God's Son. In lesson three Jesus uses scriptural replies to defeat Satan's temptations. Matthew is careful to provide great detail in how the events of Jesus' advent are the fulfillment of prophecy. The long-awaited King has arrived!

UNIT ONE: THE ADVENT OF THE KING

Lesson 1	The Arrival of the King	Matthew 1:18–2:12
Lesson 2	The Introduction of the King	Matthew 3
Lesson 3	The Temptation of the King	Matthew 4:1–11

lesson 1

The Arrival of the King

MAIN IDEA

Jesus' miraculous birth fulfilled prophecy and elicited worship.

QUESTION TO EXPLORE

How can the prophetic details of Jesus' birth affirm our faith and how should we respond to his arrival?

STUDY AIM

To comprehend the prophetic details of Jesus' birth and respond with worship

QUICK READ

Matthew's Gospel account shows how Jesus Christ perfectly fulfilled the Old Testament's prophecies about the Messiah's birth. Thus, his advent should elicit our awe and praise.

DISCOVER
BIBLE STUDY GUIDE
BELIEVE
LIVE

19

Introduction

At the height of his fame, rock musician Alice Cooper drank a bottle of whiskey daily, nearly destroying his thirty-year marriage to Sheryl. In an effort to save their relationship, he began attending church with her and felt as if God spoke to him every time. Now a believer, Cooper speaks to curious fellow musicians about his life changes. He says, "I have talked to some big stars about this, some really horrific characters, and you'd be surprised. The ones that you would think are the farthest gone are the ones that are the most apt to listen."[1]

That's probably how "religious" people viewed Matthew in first-century Galilee: too far-gone for hope or redemption. After all, as a tax collector for the Roman authorities, they regarded him as a traitor; he worked for the oppressive enemy. In all likelihood, Matthew wasn't a strict Jew either, so orthodox Israelites neither trusted nor respected him. In fact, tax collectors were often directly connected with sinners and prostitutes (Mark 2:15–16; Luke 5:30). What a reputation to live with, and somehow overcome![2]

Matthew 1:18–2:12

18 This is how the birth of Jesus Christ came about: His mother Mary was pledged to be married to Joseph, but before they came together, she was found to be with child through the Holy Spirit. **19** Because Joseph her husband was a righteous man and did not want to expose her to public disgrace, he had in mind to divorce her quietly.

20 But after he had considered this, an angel of the Lord appeared to him in a dream and said, "Joseph son of David, do not be afraid to take Mary home as your wife, because what is conceived in her is from the Holy Spirit. **21** She will give birth to a son, and you are to give him the name Jesus, because he will save his people from their sins."

22 All this took place to fulfill what the Lord had said through the prophet: **23** "The virgin will be with child and will give birth to a son, and they will call him Immanuel"—which means, "God with us."

24 When Joseph woke up, he did what the angel of the Lord had commanded him and took Mary home as his wife. **25** But he had no

Matthew 1:25

union with her until she gave birth to a son. And he gave him the name Jesus.

• • • • • • • • • • • • • • • • • • • •

¹ After Jesus was born in Bethlehem in Judea, during the time of King Herod, Magi from the east came to Jerusalem ² and asked, "Where is the one who has been born king of the Jews? We saw his star in the east and have come to worship him."

³ When King Herod heard this he was disturbed, and all Jerusalem with him. ⁴ When he had called together all the people's chief priests and teachers of the law, he asked them where the Christ was to be born. ⁵ "In Bethlehem in Judea," they replied, "for this is what the prophet has written:

⁶ "'But you, Bethlehem, in the land of Judah,
    are by no means least among the rulers of Judah;
  for out of you will come a ruler
    who will be the shepherd of my people Israel.'"

⁷ Then Herod called the Magi secretly and found out from them the exact time the star had appeared. ⁸ He sent them to Bethlehem and said, "Go and make a careful search for the child. As soon as you find him, report to me, so that I too may go and worship him."

⁹ After they had heard the king, they went on their way, and the star they had seen in the east went ahead of them until it stopped over the place where the child was. ¹⁰ When they saw the star, they were overjoyed. ¹¹ On coming to the house, they saw the child with his mother Mary, and they bowed down and worshiped him. Then they opened their treasures and presented him with gifts of gold and of incense and of myrrh. ¹² And having been warned in a dream not to go back to Herod, they returned to their country by another route.

A Little Background Information

If anyone was ever on the fringes of popular society, yet intimately involved with people from all walks of life, it was Matthew. Jesus drew him into the circle of his twelve closest disciples and transformed him into a man who abandoned wealth for austerity, perhaps even dying in Ethiopia for the gospel. But before he did, (sometime between A.D. 60–67), he wrote his account of Jesus for his own Jewish race to read. In an effort to prove Christ's veracity as the Promised Messiah, he quoted the Old Testament more than forty times and showed how Jesus fulfilled nearly twenty prophecies, more than any other Gospel writer.

Matthew even used the Jewish word "Messiah" most frequently. In fact, he never referred to Jesus by the Greek term "Christ." And, because Jews

We *Three* Kings?

The three gifts Jesus received were properly befitting one born of royalty, and although the givers probably didn't intend any symbolism, many recognize symbolism in each gift.

- *Gold*, a precious gift common for royalty, acknowledged Jesus' eternal Kingship.

- *Frankincense*, a glittering, odorous gum derived from incisions in tree bark and often used as incense in worship, recognized Jesus' divinity.

- *Myrrh* was a much-valued spice and perfume used in embalming. It foreshadowed Jesus' suffering, death, and burial; Nicodemus used it in caring for Jesus' dead body (John 19:39–40).

- Ironically, there is no specific reference to the number of individuals who presented these gifts to the infant Jesus. Thus, our traditional carol, *We Three Kings* may be inaccurate. There may have been two worshipers or dozens. Religious tradition, however, identifies them (with variations) as Melchior, Caspar, and Balthazar. The Cologne Cathedral in Germany houses a large, gilded sarcophagus called *The Shrine of the Three Kings*, which is believed to hold the bones of these three men.

Perhaps most practically, the gifts were timely. Not long after the Magi presented their treasures, Joseph, Mary, and Jesus rushed from Israel to Egypt to escape Herod's massacre of toddler boys (Matthew 2:16). These gifts probably financed the trip.

perceived the Messiah as a royal leader, more than fifty times Matthew used the word "kingdom" to describe the Son of Man's reign. But, knowing they expected an *earthly* overcomer, he usually clarified his domain as the "kingdom of heaven" to direct his readers' minds to things above (Colossians 3:2). All this was done to draw his readers into the story, and expunge any doubts about Jesus, believing these evidences would lead to Christian conversion. Without these details, Matthew's Jewish audience would consider Jesus as nothing more than an interesting guy who did some amazing things, but not the Deliverer for whom Jews had waited centuries.

Matthew began his account by reciting Jesus' legal genealogy, verifying Jesus' relation to King David and his Jewish heritage as Abraham's descendant (1:1–2), both of which were Messianic requirements. Jesus' family history was only the beginning, though. Jesus' birth was miraculous, and fulfilled prophecy that deserved recognition, reverence, and worship.

The Miraculous Arrival (1:18–25)

Jewish marriages in the first century involved a three-step process. First, legal representatives made a binding contract (usually before witnesses), covenanting to unite a man and woman (along with their families). This established the next stage, known as the betrothal, during which time the couple was legally bound, although they did not live with one another or practice marriage's intimacies.

Finally, about a year later, the couple committed themselves to one another in a formal ceremony; the bride moved in with her groom and they could engage in sexual relations. Unlike modern engagements, in which couples may nonchalantly change their minds, in Jewish culture a legal divorce was necessary to break the betrothal covenant, and it usually required a serious reason like infidelity. That is why Mary's pregnancy (1:18) was such a scandalous turn of events. Public disgrace was at risk for everyone involved. Apparently Mary (and by extension, her family) could not be trusted to hold up her end of a bargain. Furthermore, Mosaic Law stated adultery was punishable by stoning (Deuteronomy 22:23–29).

Thus, Joseph, a man "faithful to the law" (1:19) faced a difficult decision. Mary likely explained to him how she had become pregnant, but who could believe something so far-fetched, so unprecedented as a woman impregnated by the Holy Spirit? Marrying her in her obvious state might be viewed as an admission of premarital sex, risking his reputation and his standing in the local synagogue. So, he determined to avoid these risks and prevent her public humiliation by divorcing her in the presence of only two witnesses.

But God had a different plan. In a dream, an angelic messenger instructed Joseph to follow through with his commitment to Mary (1:20). In the first century, women and children depended on the presence of a mature, respected male to give them a heritage and legal voice when needed. Eight days following Jesus' birth, Joseph named the child and had him circumcised (1:25; Luke 2:21), acts done by a legal father; in essence, he adopted Jesus. Then, thirty-two days later, Joseph and Mary presented Jesus in the temple for purification (Luke 2:22–24), a further claim of paternal identification with the child. Thus, when the angel addressed Joseph as "son of David," it meant Jesus, too, would have legal ties to King David (whether by birth or adoption)—required for the Messiah.

The angel then gave Joseph the name for this divinely-conceived child (1:21). In Hebrew culture, names held great significance, pointing to the individual's actual character and destiny. The name Jesus is derived from the Hebrew *Yehosua* or *Joshua*, meaning, "Yahweh is salvation" or "God saves." Jews expected the Messiah to save Israel from Roman rule and perhaps even purify the people, but they did not expect him to give his life in order to save them from their sins. Nor did they expect him to save Gentiles, people the Jews considered heathen and outside of God's favor. When the angel said Jesus would save "his people," thoughts turned immediately to Abraham's descendants, but people of any race, nation, or tongue who would trust him by faith can be saved.

Knowing his primary audience was Jewish, Matthew made his first Old Testament reference early in his account (1:22–23). The prophecy quoted here is from Isaiah 7:14 and was spoken by the prophet to his contemporaries; however, it also had implications for future generations. Isaiah promised Judah's King Ahaz that God would bring about the birth of a royal son (perhaps Hezekiah) during whose infancy the kings of Syria and Israel would suffer ruin (Isaiah 7:16). This did not imply the royal son was also divinely conceived.

The Hebrew word *almah* used in 7:14 can be interpreted as either "young woman of marriageable age" (as in Isaiah's context) or "virgin." (However, with exceptions like Isaiah 7:14, the word primarily refers to a young woman without sexual experience.) For Jesus' mother, the verse referred to her virginity. Both the original child of 7:14 and Jesus would be called "Immanuel," which means "God with us," a statement of promise and hope about God's presence with his people. It was also a cry of dependency and confession of God's intervention on behalf of his people, whether saving them from their enemies or from their sins (see also Isa. 8:5–10).

Joseph demonstrated his faithfulness by following the angel's instructions (Matt. 1:24), risking public disgrace. He prevented further accusations that the child might be his biological son, and demonstrated strong, committed character and self-control by not having sexual relations with Mary until after Jesus' birth (Joseph and Mary later bore other children, including James, Joseph, and Jude/Judas, Simon, and sisters—see Mark 6:3). Joseph also obeyed God by naming Mary's firstborn "Jesus" (Matt. 1:25). Traditionally, sons were named after their father or a relative (Luke 1:59–61). It might have even been a demonstration of love for Joseph to name the child after himself. However, naming him Jesus was an obedient act that sealed the purpose for which this child was born.

A Little Child Stirs Up Two Kingdoms (2:1–12)

Matthew employed the next proof of Jesus' identity as Messiah by subtly referencing Old Testament prophecy concerning the Messiah's birthplace. "Bethlehem in Judea" (2:1), as distinguished from the Bethlehem in Zebulun (see Joshua 19:15), had a rich heritage for the Hebrew people. Jacob buried Rachel near this location (Genesis 35:19), and Ruth met and married Boaz near this town (Ruth 1:22–2:6)—the great-grandparents of King David. Matthew then described some unusual visitors, prophesied in Psalm 72:10–11 and Isaiah 60:3, 6.

Because these visitors from the East (probably Persia, modern-day Iraq) understood a royal child had been born, they first went to Jerusalem, the Israeli capital, to make an official "state" visit (Matt. 2:2). They were Zoroastrianists (Magi), learned people of a priestly class. They served as royal advisors because they were astrologers who faithfully studied and observed changes and unique visions in the heavens, which they believed divulged the secrets of earthly events. The star they observed was perhaps a comet, supernova, or planetary conjunction, and they believed it held significance for the Hebrew people. Because a Jewish community had settled in Babylon, the Magi were likely aware of Messianic prophecies.

Although the men came to honor the new king, Jerusalem's leaders were "disturbed," which in the Greek means "uncertain, agitated or troubled" (2:3). As a result, the population was also unsettled. Though an excellent administrator, King Herod had a reputation for instability. He was paranoid about losing his throne and executed numerous associates and family members, including his wife and at least two sons. Furthermore, the Jewish people expected the Messiah's advent to bring conflict with the ruling authorities, whomever they might be. Thus, overthrowing the Romans (as they understood the Messiah's role) probably meant war, a sobering and troubling thought.

To learn where biblical prophecy indicated the child would be born, Herod called for the high priest and others in religious authority among the Jews in Jerusalem (2:4). It is doubtful he gathered them all in one sitting, thus ensuring answers free of complicity or deceit. In verses 5–6, Matthew clearly stated the Messiah would be born in Bethlehem of Judah. Planning to eliminate this threat to his rule, Herod called the Magi privately to learn the exact time the sign appeared and sent them on to Bethlehem with instruction to report back to him, under the guise of wanting to worship as well (2:7–8).

Leaving Herod's presence, the Magi followed the star to the child (2:9–10), bowing in homage and giving him valuable gifts—fit for the royalty they believed him to be (2:11). But, because of a warning received in a dream, they returned home by another route, thus avoiding further contact or communication with Herod (2:12).

Live It Out

James 1:22 challenges believers to obey God's word, not to just hear it. Historical lessons about Christ might lead us to think there is no response necessary after studying this passage. This is false. Just as the Magi

Homework

What passages from the Old and New Testament might you share with an unbelieving friend to prove that Jesus fulfilled Messianic prophecy? See if you can locate Scriptures for the following prophecies:

- A forerunner prepared the way: Isaiah 40:3 (for example)
- Birthplace; hometown:
- Descendant of Abraham, Judah, and David:
- Born of a virgin:
- God in human form:
- Visited and honored by foreigners:
- Spent time in Egypt:
- Betrayed, falsely accused, and silent before accusers:
- Mocked and ridiculed:
- Hands and feet pierced; no bones broken:
- Clothing gambled for:
- Forsaken by God:
- Sacrifice for sin:
- Buried with the wealthy:
- Resurrected:
- Ascended into heaven and seated at God's right hand:

worshipped the Child, we too can be amazed at how God orchestrated time, space, and circumstances to bring Jesus to earth at just the right moment (Romans 5:6) to provide for humanity's salvation. Hundreds or even thousands of people could have fulfilled any number of the Messianic prophecies foretold, but only Jesus fulfilled *all of them.*

Prophets born centuries apart could not have conspired to create a collusion of descriptions to fit one man. It is awe-inspiring to consider the remarkable nature of Jesus Christ's advent. No plan of Satan, no scheme of man, could prevent his coming. Eternity was poised, ready and waiting for the arrival of this King, who was born in humble conditions and lowly circumstances. Be amazed and worship today with a full heart that is complemented by the truth of Jesus' prophetic fulfillments. And remember, that same eternal Savior sees you, loves you, and wants an intimate, personal relationship with you.

Questions

1. Did you learn anything new about Matthew or his Gospel?

2. Why is it meaningful to *you* that Jesus fulfilled Old Testament prophecy?

3. Does the fact that Jesus fulfilled prophecy strengthen your faith in the gospel message? Explain?

4. Share your thoughts about Joseph's willingness to obey the angel's commands.

5. Describe your mental image of the Magi.

6. The Magi brought precious gifts to show their honor and respect for this king. What of great value do you need to present to the Savior, perhaps something you have withheld from him?

Notes

1. Steve Beard, "The Way of Faith for Alice Cooper," *Good News Magazine* (May/June 2002), 29.

2. Unless otherwise indicated, all Scripture quotations in lessons 1–10 are from the New International Version (1984 edition).

lesson 2

The Introduction of the King

MAIN IDEA

John the Baptist's prophetic preaching prepared the way for Jesus, while Jesus' baptism confirmed his identity as God's Son.

QUESTION TO EXPLORE

How did John the Baptist and Jesus' baptism proclaim the arrival of the King?

STUDY AIM

To understand the purpose of John the Baptist's preaching and the baptism of Jesus

QUICK READ

Jesus' baptism symbolized the passing of the mantle from John the Baptist's prophetic ministry to Jesus' Messianic leadership, while simultaneously serving as Jesus' coronation and inauguration.

Introduction

We don't get a lot of ice and snow where I live. So this year, when the "ice apocalypse" hit Texas, I got stuck in Dallas, unable to make the two-hour drive home. The hotel at which I'd stayed the night before had no availability, so the concierge began an arduous search to find me a room somewhere nearby. Thankfully, someone cancelled, so I was able to stay put, but I'll never forget how hard that lady worked on my behalf. Essentially, she acted as my forerunner, going ahead of me to prepare the way for my arrival . . . somewhere!

Matthew 3

[1] In those days John the Baptist came, preaching in the Desert of Judea [2] and saying, "Repent, for the kingdom of heaven is near." [3] This is he who was spoken of through the prophet Isaiah:

"A voice of one calling in the desert,
'Prepare the way for the Lord,
　make straight paths for him.'"

[4] John's clothes were made of camel's hair, and he had a leather belt around his waist. His food was locusts and wild honey. [5] People went out to him from Jerusalem and all Judea and the whole region of the Jordan. [6] Confessing their sins, they were baptized by him in the Jordan River.

[7] But when he saw many of the Pharisees and Sadducees coming to where he was baptizing, he said to them: "You brood of vipers! Who warned you to flee from the coming wrath? [8] Produce fruit in keeping with repentance. [9] And do not think you can say to yourselves, 'We have Abraham as our father.' I tell you that out of these stones God can raise up children for Abraham. [10] The ax is already at the root of the trees, and every tree that does not produce good fruit will be cut down and thrown into the fire.

[11] "I baptize you with water for repentance. But after me will come one who is more powerful than I, whose sandals I am not fit to carry. He will baptize you with the Holy Spirit and with fire. [12] His winnowing

fork is in his hand, and he will clear his threshing floor, gathering his wheat into the barn and burning up the chaff with unquenchable fire."

13 Then Jesus came from Galilee to the Jordan to be baptized by John. **14** But John tried to deter him, saying, "I need to be baptized by you, and do you come to me?"

15 Jesus replied, "Let it be so now; it is proper for us to do this to fulfill all righteousness." Then John consented.

16 As soon as Jesus was baptized, he went up out of the water. At that moment heaven was opened, and he saw the Spirit of God descending like a dove and lighting on him. **17** And a voice from heaven said, "This is my Son, whom I love; with him I am well pleased."

The King's Forerunner (3:1–6)

After 400 years of silence, with no new messages, prophecies, or revelations from God, the Israelites were intrigued when a prophet named John suddenly burst onto the scene of first-century Judea (3:1). Preaching in the wilderness where the Jordan River flows into the Dead Sea, his designation as "the Baptist" distinguished him from other teachers with the popular name "John." His purpose was to act as the Messiah's forerunner, preparing the way for his arrival and ministry. In doing so, he called people to repent, a term meaning a radical transformation in thinking and action, from one way of life to another.

The word also carried overtones of grief. John called for this repentance because "the kingdom of heaven is near" (3:2), meaning God's reign on earth was arriving. This was an exciting announcement to a people who had long awaited his coming. However, the Jews interpreted Old Testament Messianic prophecies to mean an establishment of justice, an eradication of their enemies, and a renewal of the universe through a period of judgment. They also expected the creation of a new heaven and new earth, and a regathering of Israel under a new, united covenant. Such grand expectations would be accomplished by a mighty warrior, not a carpenter's son!

In verse 3, Matthew interjected commentary for his readers by quoting Isaiah 40:3, evidence of Old Testament prophetic fulfillment as it related to John and thus, Jesus. Isaiah claimed the Messiah's forerunner would stand in the desert, calling for people to "prepare the way for the Lord, mak[ing] straight paths for him." In ancient times, royal leaders often sent laborers ahead to make the roads clearer, smoother, and less difficult to travel. Then they followed along when the roads were ready. John's task was to make the way clear for Christ's coming by calling people to repentance. If their hearts were already inclined toward righteousness, purified by seeking forgiveness; then they would certainly be more open to receiving and believing the truths of Jesus' claims.

Similar to the prophet Elijah (2 Kings 1:8), John dressed in an animal pelt. Like others in poverty, he consumed a minimalist—if not ascetic—diet of locusts and wild honey. His novelty was undoubtedly intriguing, drawing people to the southeastern wilderness from Jerusalem, Judea, and the whole Jordan region (Matt. 3:4–5). While there, many people confessed their sins and submitted to baptism by full immersion in the Jordan River (3:6). Baptism was generally regarded as a rite reserved for Gentiles entering the Jewish faith, so it is somewhat remarkable for Jews to concede to this symbolic practice. It shows the power of the Holy Spirit working through John and the persuasiveness of his preaching and teaching. Probably his announcement of the coming kingdom was the impetus for change for some who heard him.

A Message of Action (3:7–12)

John's audience included many of the primary religious leaders of the day: both Pharisees and Sadducees (3:7). The Pharisees were scribes and lawyers who rigorously obeyed the Mosaic Law and all the other thousands of man-made (Pharisaic) laws, and they expected complete adherence by everyone else. Because they were closely connected to the local synagogues, they were more popular with most people, unlike their counterparts the Sadducees, who were generally wealthy, aristocratic priests with power and influence because of their role in the temple and Sanhedrin.

Perhaps some of these religious leaders came to see John because of curiosity or to appease the crowds, but most came to listen to him to validate or investigate his ministry. Many responded in anger. John's words, therefore, were neither complimentary nor respectful. Instead of honoring the religious elite by calling them "Rabbi," John called them "vipers"—small, dangerous snakes known for their long, hinged fangs that injected venom. John challenged these leaders with a rhetorical question that essentially asked, "Do you think being here or being baptized will save you from the coming Day of Judgment even though you are non-repentant?"

John called for true inward change rather than simply a reformation of outward behaviors (3:8). Merely following the correct procedures didn't necessarily give evidence of a pure heart. John also warned the many Jews who mistakenly trusted their ethnicity and family lineage as their source for salvation (3:9). They believed it merited them a guarantee of God's promises, regardless of their beliefs or behaviors. John's warning was ominous: those who are not pure internally, producing good fruit externally, will not last (3:10).

The repentance for which John baptized was intended to prepare people to welcome the Messiah and receive his message of salvation and *his* baptism. John knew he could not offer the salvation the Messiah would bring, thus, he humbly identified himself as submissive to Christ (see also John 3:30). He would not bring the kingdom of God, nor could he will the Holy

Preaching the Kingdom is Near

When referring to God's reign, Mark, Luke, and John prefer the term "kingdom of God." Although Matthew used that expression four times (12:28; 19:24; 21:31, 43), he preferred the description "kingdom of heaven" (used thirty-one times in the NIV).

Matthew did not intend to restrict the extent of God's sovereignty to heaven, exclusive of the earth or any other place. There are enough parallel passages between the Gospels to indicate Matthew meant the same thing as the other writers (Matt. 4:17 and Mark 1:14–15; Matt. 5:3 and Luke 6:20). Is there a reason why only he chose to use this phrase?

The most likely explanation is Mathew avoided "kingdom of God" to prevent offending Jews (his primary audience) who refused to speak or write God's holy name for fear of breaking the third commandment (Exodus 20:7). In fact, Jews often used substitute words like "heaven" to refer to God (Daniel 4:26); in literature, they omitted the letters of God's name (YAHWEH=YHWH) to avoid vain misuse.

Spirit to act. The Messiah, though, would cleanse hearts and lives, purifying and purging them with a refinement akin to fire. The repentant would be given the blessing of the Holy Spirit, but the unrepentant would be judged with eternal fire.

John elaborated with an analogy familiar to his Palestinian audience. At the end of the harvest, the "winnowing fork" was used to throw the mixed wheat and chaff into the air. Usually done on high ground during a good wind, the process separated the lighter chaff from the heavier wheat. The threshing floor was then cleared: the wheat put into storage to be milled as flour for making bread, and the chaff became fuel for fire (3:11–12).

The King's Baptism (3:13–17)

Regardless of opposition or commendation, John continued his ministry obediently. Up to this point, Matthew's narrative had been more descriptive in nature, but now Jesus entered the story for the first time as an adult, coming to John for baptism (3:13). This unsettled John. Although John's Gospel seems to indicate the Baptizer didn't know he'd immersed the Messiah until after he baptized Jesus (1:31–34), clearly John perceived something in Jesus' nature or character which indicated he did not need repentance from sin.

Certainly his parents told him of Mary's visit to Elizabeth thirty years earlier (Luke 1:39–45), so he had heard Jesus' birth was even more miraculous than his own. Whatever the insight, John tried to stop Jesus from seeking baptism and instead requested baptism for himself—whether by water or the Holy Spirit is uncertain. It is ironic that John had denied the religious leaders baptism because of their unworthiness, and yet here, John struggled to baptize Jesus because John felt unworthy.

Jesus' explanation is cryptic (3:15), but it expressed his desire to fulfill his mission. His statement simultaneously endorsed John's ministry, yet also took the mantle of leadership from John. Jesus' immersion would identify him with humanity and our need for freedom from sin. Thus, in his first recorded words in Matthew's Gospel, Jesus said to John "let it be so now" or "permit it immediately." He didn't want to waste time. John consented because Jesus said his baptism was "proper," which carries the idea of being right, appropriate, or fitting.

Believer's Baptism

Baptism's root word, *bapto*, literally means, "to dip." This is why many churches fully immerse individuals, believing this to be the most accurate imitation of the baptism described in the New Testament. In fact, in many ancient churches, baptisteries were cut into the ground in the shape of a cross, and participants extended their arms when lying down in the water symbolizing Christ's death (and their own death to sin), then rising again to signify Christ's resurrection and their new life. Because the New Testament shows no specific evidence of infant baptism, many traditions and denominations offer baptism only to those who proclaim *verbally* their faith in Christ, which would exclude infants.

Because of Jesus' obedience, we see God express his pleasure visibly. After Jesus came out of the water, heaven was opened up and God's Spirit descended like a dove, landing on Jesus. This was accompanied by a voice from heaven saying, "This is my Son, whom I love; with him I am well pleased" (3:16–17).

The language here is a bit tricky for modern interpretation, especially when paralleled with John's account of the same experience (John 1:29–34). Matthew and Mark (1:1–11) imply *either* John or Jesus saw the Spirit of God descend like a dove; Luke (3:21–22) just acknowledges it happened, and John quoted the Baptizer as having observed the phenomenon. Furthermore, did the writers mean the Spirit's manner of descent was *like* a dove's or that the Spirit appeared in the physical form of a dove? Scholars simply do not know. Regardless, the Holy Spirit's arrival is not to be understood as Jesus receiving the Spirit for the first time during this episode.

Another point of uncertainty concerns the audience of this heavenly testimony. Whereas Mark and Luke used second person pronouns, meaning the voice spoke directly to Jesus ("*You* are my Son;" "with *you* I am well pleased"), Matthew used third person pronouns ("*this* is my Son;" "with *him* I am well pleased"). John declared the Baptizer saw and heard everything. Thus, readers are left to presume at least both John and Jesus—and probably others—witnessed the heavenly voice express pleasure and delight. It is also important to note that either use of pronouns is a quotation of Old

Testament Messianic prophecy. Mark and Luke may have been referencing Psalm 2:7, while Matthew could have been harkening back to Isaiah 42:1, 2 Samuel 7:13–14, or Psalm 89:27–29.

Ultimately, it doesn't matter who heard the voice; more important is that the voice spoke and what was said. No longer was God quiet (Isaiah 42:14); he spoke, revealing himself to humanity and indicating the arrival of the Redeemer. This was the One for whom the world was waiting, even if many didn't know it. Assuming John heard the voice, it may have helped confirm his suspicions about Jesus' identity as the Messiah and his decision to follow through with baptizing Jesus.

Live It Out

Ancient kings had people who cleared paths and announced their coming; that is precisely what John did as the Messiah's forerunner. He begged his listening audience to ready their hearts for Jesus to step into their souls and take residence and authority. Although it was an unorthodox method by which to introduce a king, John's baptism of Christ did exactly that. Coupled with the crowning presence of the Holy Spirit, this episode in Jesus' life served as his coronation, confirming his identity as God's Son, even though few others around him knew the significance of the occasion.

You and I are blessed with that same presence of the Holy Spirit when we receive the atoning and substitutionary death of Christ on our behalf. He seals us as God's children (Ephesians 4:30 and Romans 8:16), a royal priesthood and special possession (1 Peter 2:9). Although Baptists don't believe baptism saves us or prompts the arrival of the Holy Spirit, we do believe it models the life, death, and resurrection of our Savior. It also symbolizes the change Christ is making internally. Jesus didn't *need* baptism, but he did it anyway. Consider today if you should follow his example.

Questions

1. Why do you think believers should consider being baptized? What difference has it made in your life or in the life of someone you know? List any excuses you've given or heard from others about why baptism is unnecessary.

2. Discuss any known requirements for baptism in your local church body (complete a new believer's class, meet a minimum age requirement, etc.).

3. How do you think you would have addressed or dealt with the Pharisees and Sadducees if you had been John?

4. How do you see Jesus' immersion as a means of identifying with humanity and our need for freedom from sin?

5. What is your response to someone who, in a different faith tradition, has been sprinkled or was baptized as an infant? What would you say to someone who was physically unable to be immersed, but wanted to be baptized as evidence of their new faith in Christ?

6. Do you think others beside Jesus and John heard God's audible testimony about Jesus? Explain.

FOCAL TEXT

Matthew 4:1–11

BACKGROUND

Matthew 4:1–11

lesson 3

The Temptation of the King

MAIN IDEA

Jesus defeated temptation with scriptural replies to Satan's snares.

QUESTION TO EXPLORE

What can we learn from Jesus about defeating temptation?

STUDY AIM

To become convinced that the key to defeating temptation is knowing and obeying God's word

QUICK READ

Jesus' temptations reveal a loyalty to the Father and a keen knowledge of Scripture. We have the privilege of responding to temptation with the same dependent strength on God's power.

DISCOVER

BIBLE STUDY GUIDE

BELIEVE

LIVE

Introduction

If sinning wasn't fun, it wouldn't tempt us. If sin didn't challenge our desires and cravings, we wouldn't need to discuss how to overcome it. I have never met a person who has struggled with an addiction to Brussels sprouts, or couldn't be pried away from a visit to the proctologist's office. However, I have known many people who cannot resist a visit to their favorite pornography site. Their spiritual lives suffer from such decisions. Others cannot resist a juicy piece of gossip, and their sin undermines, sabotages, and mutilates others' reputation and future. You've probably watched those whose bodies, minds, or both deteriorated from drug or alcohol addiction, and have seen their families and lives destroyed.

Temptation is real. It is powerful, and when given into, it's deadly. That's why Satan uses such enticements as a primary tool to destroy us mentally, physically, emotionally, and spiritually. Matthew 4 indicates he sought to destroy our Savior, too.

Matthew 4:1–11

[1] Then Jesus was led by the Spirit into the desert to be tempted by the devil. [2] After fasting forty days and forty nights, he was hungry. [3] The tempter came to him and said, "If you are the Son of God, tell these stones to become bread."

[4] Jesus answered, "It is written: 'Man does not live on bread alone, but on every word that comes from the mouth of God.'"

[5] Then the devil took him to the holy city and had him stand on the highest point of the temple. [6] "If you are the Son of God," he said, "throw yourself down. For it is written:

"'He will command his angels concerning you,
    and they will lift you up in their hands,
    so that you will not strike your foot against a stone.'"

[7] Jesus answered him, "It is also written: 'Do not put the Lord your God to the test.'"

[8] Again, the devil took him to a very high mountain and showed him all the kingdoms of the world and their splendor. [9] "All this I will give you," he said, "if you will bow down and worship me."

> ¹⁰ Jesus said to him, "Away from me, Satan! For it is written: 'Worship the Lord your God, and serve him only.'"
> ¹¹ Then the devil left him, and angels came and attended him.

What We Want—Physical Desires (4:1–4)

Following the exaltation of his baptism at which the Holy Spirit anointed him as God's ordained Son, the Holy Spirit then led Jesus out to the wilderness to be tempted (4:1). God did not tempt Jesus (see James 1:13); the devil did. The Greek word for "devil" is *diabolos*, a term meaning "accuser" or "slanderer;" he is certainly our enemy and adversary.

For forty days, Jesus fasted from food (4:2). Fasting served multiple purposes in ancient faith practice. People fasted publicly or privately, either abstaining from food completely or partially (from specific foods) for a variety of reasons: as an expression of bereavement (1 Samuel 31:11–13; 2 Samuel 1:11–12); confession (Psalm 69:10); distress (Esther 4:3; 1 Sam. 20:34; Daniel 6:18; Acts 27:33); and penitence (Nehemiah 9:1–3; Joel 1:13–14; Jonah 3:5–9). God's people also fasted as they prayed and sought God's intervention (2 Sam. 12:15–17; 2 Chronicles 20:2–4; Ezra 8:21); guidance (Judges 20:26–28; Dan. 9:3, 10:2–12); or for a deeper experience with God (Isaiah 58; Zechariah 7:5).

As a result of his fast, Jesus was absolutely famished when Satan chose to attack. That is just like the devil—he tempts us at our weakest moments, when we're less capable of making wise decisions, and when we are most likely to act out of emotion or convenience. At this moment, Satan appealed to Jesus' most urgent and basic need: food. He said, "If you are the Son of God, tell these stones to become bread" (Matt. 4:3).

The English translation appears to question Jesus' identity, but the Greek indicative for "if" means "since" or "because." Satan, therefore, asked Jesus to question the meaning of his earthly role as God's Son, not his deity. God had just declared his pleasure in him (3:17); Satan was already attempting to make Jesus doubt his strength to undergo the rigors of human life and God's ability to empower his journey. After all, surely, as God's Son, Jesus had the right to a bit of sustenance.

Hebrews 4:15 declares that Jesus was tempted in every way we are. This first temptation is representative of our effort to fulfill any of our physical desires in improper ways. Whether we crave food, sexual intimacy, emotional connection, health and well-being, a certain bodily ideal, or even fun, rarely are our desires wrong or evil. How we go about satisfying them is what gets us into trouble; whether through excess, deprivation, or by going outside of God's prescribed boundaries.

Bread is certainly a basic need for humanity. Its carbohydrates provide energy to strengthen and sustain basic involuntary bodily functions. Satan challenged the Son of God to perform a self-satisfying miracle. Yet, Jesus' calling was to perform miracles on behalf of others (feeding of the 5000, healings from infirmities, etc.), not to gratify his own fleshly desires. He deferred his own satiation in favor of choosing the sustenance of God's pleasure (4:4). His powers as God were not limited because he chose not to use them in this moment of temptation; rather, his strength of character, meekness, resolve, and purpose were distinctly revealed.

Could Jesus *really* live at peace with limitations as a human being? Could he deny himself the basic right of food to sustain him? The fully human part of Jesus had to submit to God's directives just like all followers. Thus, his reply in Matthew 4:4 was a quote from Deuteronomy 8:3. God's utterances bring life, and Jesus firmly stated his trust in God's sustenance as enough, even more, than he could provide for himself.

What We Crave—Position and Control (4:5–7)

Hoping to draw Jesus into a prideful debate or sinful behavior, Satan took Jesus in a vision, standing him on the highest point of the temple complex in Jerusalem (4:5–6). Jews perceived the temple as a place of divine safety because God dwelled within; here Satan challenged Jesus to prove his identity as God's Son. Yet in this second temptation, Satan employed an additional tactic. He quoted Psalm 91:11–12 to "validate" his challenge (4:6). Since Jesus used Scripture to combat the first test, the devil used Scripture (out of context) to extend his next challenge. If Jesus threw himself down from this lofty location, wasn't God obligated to save him? Wasn't Jesus entitled to such preservation? And what about the public spectacle it might create—wouldn't it put Jesus in the limelight?

Fundamentally, this temptation addressed pride, because people want so often to prove their worth, role, or strength. We don't want to be thought of or perceived as less than we are (or less than we *think* we are). Pride causes a desire to control people's perceptions, to obtain their approval, to avoid disappointing them, and to avoid rejection. Satan hoped Jesus felt an arrogant need to "prove himself" as God's Son. To do so at that point would have been the wrong timing and in the wrong manner. God sent Jesus to be a suffering servant, not a spectacular showman. Jesus didn't need to prove to others what he already knew to be true: he *is* God's Son and God. At an even more basic level, this temptation questioned the wisdom of God's plan for reconciling the world to himself. Surely a sensational and dramatic display would garner more attention, a greater following, and circumvent the need for the cross.

Temptation and Addiction

When temptation is not met with discipline, it can grow into an addiction. We think overcoming addiction should be a simple matter of saying no to a tempting situation. However, addiction is a disease that is often biological or genetic. For example, in the case of pornography, neurological studies now reveal that during sexual stimulation, neurons in the brain involuntarily begin planning how to mimic the behaviors observed, triggering sexual tension. Meanwhile, the brain produces the neurochemical dopamine, which reinforces reward-motivated behavior. As a result, when viewing or reading pornographic material, our bodies release hormone reinforcement, and we form attachments to images and not spouses.[1]

We must also see addiction on a spiritual level: 1) a constant, bombarding attack by the enemy to steal, kill, and destroy (John 10:10); and 2) a failed attempt to find peace and satisfaction outside of God. Treating addiction requires a multifaceted approach. Treatment must include therapy, physical rehabilitation, education, and other elements, including spiritual growth. Just saying no is not enough; the addictive behavior must be replaced with alternatives, such as time in God's word, prayer, and actively serving God.

Using Scripture out of context manipulates it in order to justify sinful behavior and circumvent holy behavior. Jesus' reply, a quotation of Deuteronomy 6:16, firmly opposed Satan's suggestion and refused to allow him to misuse or interpret Scripture for his own purposes. To execute such a sensational spectacle would, in effect, force God's hand. Although God is certainly capable of handling any situation, to insist God prove his faithfulness is absurd. Jesus had no doubts about God's ability or willingness to protect him, nor should we. In fact, Satan never assumed nor suggested God would allow Jesus' destruction. It became a question of pride about who was right and trustworthy and who was not.

Pride and independent self-reliance says, "Only I know the best plan and can best meet my own needs." Dependent trust says, "God's faithfulness is a known quantity; he is with me and for me, even if things don't happen the way I think they should or don't look or feel right to me." To test God (as Satan suggested) is to challenge God's character in a disrespectful and unloving way. He is not afraid of our questions; he welcomes them. But as a holy God, he deserves reverence, even in our frustration and struggle. Jesus refuted Satan's temptation and held firm in his belief in God's faithful plan and provision, refusing to test God. By refusing to jump, Jesus chose the path of continuing danger and hardship.

What We Desire—Power and Possessions (4:8–11)

Lastly, in another vision, Satan took Jesus to a very high mountain, presenting the world's kingdoms and their splendor, but not their sinfulness (4:8). As they gazed at God's creation, Satan offered Jesus all the power and possessions therein if he would humbly worship him (4:9). Satan's proposition, however ridiculous (why would Creator God worship his created being?), offered Jesus the temporary over the eternal. Jesus knew this world will pass away (1 Corinthians 7:31; 1 John 2:17). Earthly royal and political kingdoms do not last forever, and vast treasures cannot compare to heaven's glorious riches (Ephesians 1:18; 3:16; Revelation 21:10–21). Jesus had to choose the "unseen best" over the "visible good."

It seems as though Satan offered Jesus something that didn't even belong to him in this temptation. Although Jesus created the world with God and

When Facing Temptation

Consider these practical steps to responding to temptation:

- Focus on the big picture, not just the immediate pleasure.

- Remember God is faithful (1 Cor. 10:13).

- Rely on the power of the Holy Spirit (Phil. 4:13, Acts 1:8a).

- Set your mind on things above, including Scripture and worship (Col. 3:2, 1 John 2:15–17).

- Identify areas of weakness; know your limitations.

- Recognize times of weakness. Remember H.A.L.T.: don't make decisions when you are Hungry, Angry, Lonely, or Tired.

- Build a defense by knowing God's word (Joshua 1:8; Ps. 119:11).

- Be in accountable relationships with people who will encourage you to seek God.

as God (John 1:1–4; Genesis 1:1; Job 38:4); Jesus knew the world and its kingdoms were nevertheless under Satan's power temporarily (John 12:31; 2 Corinthians 4:4; Eph. 2:2; 6:12). The people in those kingdoms were the very people he left the glories of heaven to redeem. However, following his obedience on the cross and his resurrection, Jesus announced, "All authority in heaven and on earth has been given to me" (Matt. 28:18).

Jesus' reply to Satan in Matthew 4:10, quoting Deuteronomy 6:13, not only refused to worship anyone but God, but also rejected any shortcut to achieving the kingdom that would one day be his. Jesus would not compromise his loyalty to the Father, even if it meant enduring the coming pain, abandonment, and agony of the cross.

Subsequent to Jesus' direct and unwavering command to depart from him, Satan left Jesus' presence and angels came to minister to him, just as Psalm 91:11–12 states. Matthew 4:11 implies that these heavenly messengers provided both physical sustenance and emotional and spiritual comfort to Jesus (cf. Heb. 1:6), and further established Jesus' identity as God's Son for the benefit of Matthew's readers. However, this temptation was the first of many confrontations Jesus would have with Satan's presence and power, for the true King was now invading the enemy's domain, and he had learned how to resist the devil.

Live It Out

We are subject to the same kinds of temptations Jesus experienced, with every derivation and aspect of those yearnings. Fundamentally–from the first in Genesis 3 until now—every temptation asks: *Does God really know best? Is he really good? Will he keep his promises?*

Jesus averted Satan's attempts to undermine his life and ministry because he rebutted him with Scripture, and we can do the same when our enemy comes seeking to kill and destroy us (John 10:10). You and I cannot outwit the cunning Satan, but we can command him to flee, and he must (see James 4:7). In John 14:30–31, Jesus said that Satan, "has no hold over me, but he comes so that the world may learn that I love the Father and do exactly what my Father has commanded me." Our temptations provide opportunities for God to show his power in our lives. Ultimately, the root of temptation is the decision to choose whom we will worship: God (trusting his character and authority), or ourselves (opting for our own preferences and logic). How will you respond to temptation today?

Questions

1. When are you most vulnerable to temptation?

2. Recall a time when you combatted temptation with Scripture or identify a recent temptation and a Scripture you could have used to overcome it.

3. What are your greatest physical temptations? Be specific.

4. What steps can you take to quell pride, arrogance, and the need for others' acceptance?

5. How has Satan tempted you to circumvent the journey God has planned for you so you could take an easier route?

6. What new insights about Jesus' temptation did the Holy Spirit reveal to you through this lesson?

Notes

1. William M. Struthers, Pornography Addiction in the Brain: Its Destructive Nature and How To Overcome It, http://enrichmentjournal.ag.org/201103/201103_080_porn_addict.cfm. Accessed 4/30/2015.

UNIT TWO
The Manifesto of the King

Unit Two, "The Manifesto of the King" contains four lessons that address the content of the Sermon on the Mount found in Matthew 5–7. In these lessons we see Jesus interpreting many of the Old Testament teachings in light of his arrival as the promised Messiah and King. His sermon illustrates what life is to be like in the kingdom of God as he defines the attitudes and behaviors kingdom citizens should possess. Jesus assures his listeners he has not come to abolish the law, but to fulfill it. Lesson four focuses on the Beatitudes, which outline the path to being fully satisfied in Christ. Lesson five addresses how we are to understand the Old Testament Law and Prophets in light of Jesus' coming. Lesson six describes how citizens in God's kingdom should concentrate on making eternal investments, trusting him to meet their needs. Lesson seven reveals that life in God's kingdom requires spiritual discernment.

FOCAL TEXT	BACKGROUND
Matthew 5:1–12	Matthew 5:1–12

lesson 4

Secrets to Full Satisfaction

MAIN IDEA

The Beatitudes outline the path to being fully satisfied in Christ.

QUESTION TO EXPLORE

How can we become fully satisfied in Christ?

STUDY AIM

To choose to exhibit the character described in the Beatitudes as my path to satisfaction in Christ

QUICK READ

Jesus encouraged those who were suffering to be satisfied by looking beyond their circumstances to God, who was aware of them, cared for them, and would bless their humility.

DISCOVER
BELIEVE
LIVE

BIBLE STUDY GUIDE

Introduction

The band The Rolling Stones, sings the song "Satisfaction." The theme of the song is that satisfaction remains elusive, no matter how hard we try to obtain it. That song could be used to describe many people today. The world offers a variety of solutions to the search for satisfaction, but every one of them is incomplete and temporary. Only Jesus offers lasting and fulfilling satisfaction. This kind of satisfaction is not negated by difficult circumstances, but instead gains strength during trying times.

The Gospel of Matthew contains Jesus' Sermon on the Mount, and chapters 5 thru 7 contain more than just one of Jesus' sermons. His messages focused on how to live a righteous life in a secular society. This section of Scripture opens with a series of blessings and ends with a series of warnings, a pattern also found in the Book of Deuteronomy. This allusion to the Old Testament connected Moses and Jesus as the mediators of God's commandments.

The blessings in Matthew 5 are known as "beatitudes." A "beatitude" is a declaration that confers a blessing on the person who lives according to God's principles. Both the Psalms and the Book of Proverbs contain the majority of Old Testament beatitudes. The original word for "blessed" in Matthew 5 can be translated as "fully satisfied." The Beatitudes contradicted the belief of religious leaders that the educated would be first in the kingdom of God, and the poor would be last. Jesus made it clear that God would bless those who came to him with empty hands, not those who thought they could impress God.

Matthew 5:1–12

1 Now when he saw the crowds, he went up on a mountainside and sat down. His disciples came to him, 2 and he began to teach them, saying:

3 "Blessed are the poor in spirit, for theirs is the kingdom of heaven.

4 Blessed are those who mourn, for they will be comforted.

5 Blessed are the meek, for they will inherit the earth.

> [6] Blessed are those who hunger and thirst for righteousness, for they will be filled.
> [7] Blessed are the merciful, for they will be shown mercy.
> [8] Blessed are the pure in heart, for they will see God.
> [9] Blessed are the peacemakers, for they will be called sons of God.
> [10] Blessed are those who are persecuted because of righteousness, for theirs is the kingdom of heaven.
> [11] "Blessed are you when people insult you, persecute you and falsely say all kinds of evil against you because of me. [12] Rejoice and be glad, because great is your reward in heaven, for in the same way they persecuted the prophets who were before you.

Blessed Are Those Who Suffer (5:3–6)

Jesus began his sermon not by condemning sinners, but rather by pronouncing blessings on those who suffer in different ways, first by speaking to those in the crowd who were "poor in spirit" (5:3). The majority of people listening to Jesus that day were poor economically. Their financial situation affected their emotional state. People without employment often have no choice but to beg for money or food. The act of begging takes an enormous emotional toll on an individual. The result was a poverty of spirit.

The culture in Jesus' day did not consider those poor people as blessed. It did not recognize the value of a person despite the person's job or economic status (much like our culture today). The poor in spirit did not lack faith, but rather acknowledged their spiritual need. It is more difficult to recognize spiritual or emotional need when all of our physical and financial needs are met. Those who were poor in spirit were the opposite of the haughty and self-sufficient. These people recognized they were bankrupt spiritually (and financially) and needed God.

To be poor in spirit is to realize you have nothing and can do nothing, and therefore you are in need of everything. Those who are poor in spirit admit their utter helplessness. Jesus proclaimed that those who acknowledge their need for God would receive the kingdom of God. This first beatitude, along with the last, are the only two that speak of receiving an immediate blessing.

3-4-2018

The other blessings conferred on those whom Jesus mentioned would be realized at a later time.

The second blessing Jesus pronounced focused on those who mourned. The word used for mourning referred to "a loud wailing" and was the strongest Greek term used for this deep sadness. Many things can cause mourning—personal sin, loss, oppression, or social concerns, just to name a few. Those listening to Jesus' teaching understood loss and suffering. The average life expectancy was twenty-five years, so losing a loved one was common. In addition, Israel suffered under Roman rule and the nation longed to be free. Jesus did not define the source of mourning, but the context suggests his promise applied to all mourning.

God promised to personally comfort those who mourned. They would experience some comfort in their current lives, but their grief would ultimately find relief one day in the kingdom of God. Jesus told them God was present in their suffering; one day he would wipe away their tears forever.

3) The third group of people Jesus blessed was the meek. The traditional meaning of the word "meek" is "gentleness or soft." However, Jesus' use of the word was more akin to Psalm 37:11, where the word for meek meant "powerlessness; the inability of a person to move his or her life forward." Jesus used the state of meekness to explain that the poor and oppressed, not the rich rulers, would inherit the earth. The word for "earth" also means "land." Those who mourn would receive the land of covenant promise. Although the poor could not purchase houses, livestock, and land, one day God would give them the land he promised to the Israelite people—the kingdom of God.

humble

4) Next, Jesus blessed those who "hunger and thirst for righteousness, for they will be filled" (Matt. 5:6). Jesus combined the words hunger and thirst for emphasis and scope. All of his listeners had experienced hunger and thirst at some point. Jesus used these words to show the intensity of those who seek righteousness. Those who hungered and thirsted for righteousness yearned to see God's standards established and obeyed. The word Matthew used for "righteousness" can also refer to justice. Due to the absence of justice in their world, many of those listening experienced hunger and thirst. Jesus promised that the people affected by injustice would be filled. The wrongs done against them would be eradicated, and God would vindicate

them. God would not only satisfy their physical hunger and thirst, but he would also mete out justice on behalf of those who had been oppressed.

Blessed Are Those Who Treat People Right (5:7–9)

Jesus turned his comments to those who had the opportunity to make a difference among the suffering. He proclaimed that those who show love and kindness would be shown mercy. Jesus used a word for mercy that has Old Testament connections to the Hebrew word *hesed*. *Hesed* has no equivalent in the English language. It was used to describe the covenantal love God has for his people. God's mercy is not received by merit; rather it is given out of loving-kindness and compassion. Mercy is granted even if the person receiving it never asks for it or deserves it. God's mercy, not human mercy, is promised to those who are merciful. The merciful may not receive kindness from others, but God promised to show them his mercy, a grace and kindness much richer and satisfying than any kindness a person could offer.

Next, Jesus promised that the pure in heart would see God (5:8). The religious leaders of that day emphasized outward demonstrations of purity. However, such purity was fake and insincere. Purity begins in the heart and

Blessed

The word "blessed" occurs fifty-five times in the New Testament. Over time, it has become associated with Christian thought. However, the word has secular roots even before Jesus' day. It was typically used to describe outward prosperity and was connected to wealth. In Greek culture, the gods were considered "blessed" because of their power and prestige. The word was used to reveal the superiority of the gods over people, but their superiority was due to their force and intellect, not their morality. Philosophers began to use the word to describe a person who was prosperous, yet knowledgeable and wise. This definition attached morality to the word. Christian thought moved the meaning of the word "blessed" from outward prosperity to inward character. People with integrity and a right relationship with God find true satisfaction and are therefore considered blessed.

A Path to Peacemaking

When people hurl insults, persecute, or say false things about you:

1. Do not retaliate.
2. Do not lose hope.
3. Do not grumble and complain.
4. Live a life that demonstrates your faith in Christ.
5. Trust your current struggles to your Savior who promises an eventual and eternal reward.

then is manifested in outward behavior. The heart represents the center of a person, the place from which a person feels, thinks, and makes choices. Those who demonstrate a lifestyle of purity that mirrors an inward purity would see God, not the priests whose pious actions did not mirror the true condition of their hearts. The pure in heart exhibit commitment to God that comes from a heart cleansed by Jesus. People with a pure heart will "see God." The idea of the pure in heart seeing God is also found in Psalm 11:7, 17:15, and Job 19:26–27. Sin hinders a person from seeing God. Purity in heart is only possible through the regenerative work of the Holy Spirit.

Jesus also blessed peacemakers. He was challenging his listeners to be peaceable people and to try to bring peace where it does not currently exist. Jesus is the ideal peacemaker, and God's children are to follow his example. Peace is connected with justice. God's children are to cooperate with God by standing up for what is right and seeking justice for the oppressed.

Blessed Are Those Who Suffer For Doing Right (5:10–12)

In these verses, Jesus' tone changed slightly as he warned his followers they would be mistreated. Persecution is a mark of those who follow Jesus. The world does not always honor those who do the right thing, but God does. Many people suffer for various reasons (poverty, abuse, illness, etc.), but

Jesus blessed those who suffer because of their commitment to him and to righteousness. This blessing was directed to people who actively pursued righteousness and were mistreated for it.

In this pronouncement, Jesus revealed for the first time that connection to him is necessary to see the coming kingdom of God. Jesus connected suffering for following him with suffering for doing the right thing. He indicated the hardships he discussed would continue and even intensify. Jesus told his followers not to panic when people slandered them because of their connection to him. Rather, his followers should rejoice because suffering would bring great reward in heaven.

Live It Out

Jesus offended people in his day, just like he offends people even today. His warning to his followers also applies to us. Those who follow Jesus should not be surprised when they face persecution and opposition for their commitment to Christ. In fact, believers should expect it. Like the followers of Jesus' day, believers today can rejoice, knowing God is aware of their suffering and has a huge reward waiting for them in heaven.

As followers of Jesus, we have an opportunity to influence society and the lives of those around us. People may not notice or appreciate the differences we make, and that is OK. Our joy comes from knowing God notices, and he will reward us for our suffering and our acts of righteousness that come from an inward transformation.

Questions

1. Jesus intended for the Beatitudes to be understood as marks and characteristics of each disciple in their present, daily lives. How does one assist members of our contemporary culture to understand and apply these characteristics?"

2. How has suffering affected your relationship with Jesus?

3. Hunger and thirst can be intense. How do you demonstrate that same intensity for righteousness in your life?

4. How can you carry out meekness in your daily routine?

5. What are some things you can do to be a peacemaker in your community?

6. How have you been persecuted for following Jesus?

lesson  5

Fulfilling the Law of the Kingdom

MAIN IDEA

Jesus did not come to abolish the Old Testament Law or Prophets, but to fulfill them.

QUESTION TO EXPLORE

How are we to understand the Old Testament Law and Prophets in light of Jesus' coming?

STUDY AIM

To comprehend how Jesus fulfilled the Old Testament Law and Prophets and what this means for my life today

QUICK READ

Jesus told his listeners that he did not come to abolish the Law but rather to fulfill it. He explained different aspects of the Law and how his followers should live them out.

59

Introduction

Here are some unusual Texas laws:
- You must acknowledge a supreme being before holding public office.
- Criminals must give their victims twenty-four-hour notice of their intentions, either orally or in writing, and to explain the nature of the crime to be committed.
- It is illegal to sell your eye.

Some laws have been created as a reaction to changing culture and the behavior of people within it. While some laws still apply today, some no longer matter, and while still officially "on the books," those laws are no longer enforced. Other laws are replaced with newer, more appropriate ones.

Ironically, the religious leaders of Jesus' day were the mediators of God's laws. They followed only the laws that suited them, but often ignored or found loopholes in the portions they didn't like. In this section of Scripture, Jesus highlighted some common laws of his day, and called his followers to follow the spirit of those laws. He interpreted these laws in light of his arrival as Messiah and King, stating he had not come to obliterate the laws, but to fulfill them.

Matthew 5:17–48

[17] "Do not think that I have come to abolish the Law or the Prophets; I have not come to abolish them but to fulfill them. [18] I tell you the truth, until heaven and earth disappear, not the smallest letter, not the least stroke of a pen, will by any means disappear from the Law until everything is accomplished. [19] Anyone who breaks one of the least of these commandments and teaches others to do the same will be called least in the kingdom of heaven, but whoever practices and teaches these commands will be called great in the kingdom of heaven. [20] For I tell you that unless your righteousness surpasses that of the Pharisees and the teachers of the law, you will certainly not enter the kingdom of heaven.

[21] "You have heard that it was said to the people long ago, 'Do not murder, and anyone who murders will be subject to judgment.' [22] But

I tell you that anyone who is angry with his brother will be subject to judgment. Again, anyone who says to his brother, 'Raca,' is answerable to the Sanhedrin. But anyone who says, 'You fool!' will be in danger of the fire of hell. 23 "Therefore, if you are offering your gift at the altar and there remember that your brother has something against you, 24 leave your gift there in front of the altar. First go and be reconciled to your brother; then come and offer your gift. 25 "Settle matters quickly with your adversary who is taking you to court. Do it while you are still with him on the way, or he may hand you over to the judge, and the judge may hand you over to the officer, and you may be thrown into prison. 26 I tell you the truth, you will not get out until you have paid the last penny.

27 "You have heard that it was said, 'Do not commit adultery.' 28 But I tell you that anyone who looks at a woman lustfully has already committed adultery with her in his heart. 29 If your right eye causes you to sin, gouge it out and throw it away. It is better for you to lose one part of your body than for your whole body to be thrown into hell. 30 And if your right hand causes you to sin, cut it off and throw it away. It is better for you to lose one part of your body than for your whole body to go into hell.

31 "It has been said, 'Anyone who divorces his wife must give her a certificate of divorce.' 32 But I tell you that anyone who divorces his wife, except for marital unfaithfulness, causes her to become an adulteress, and anyone who marries the divorced woman commits adultery.

33 "Again, you have heard that it was said to the people long ago, 'Do not break your oath, but keep the oaths you have made to the Lord.' 34 But I tell you, Do not swear at all: either by heaven, for it is God's throne; 35 or by the earth, for it is his footstool; or by Jerusalem, for it is the city of the Great King. 36 And do not swear by your head, for you cannot make even one hair white or black. 37 Simply let your 'Yes' be 'Yes,' and your 'No,' 'No'; anything beyond this comes from the evil one.

38 "You have heard that it was said, 'Eye for eye, and tooth for tooth.' 39 But I tell you, Do not resist an evil person. If someone strikes you on the right cheek, turn to him the other also. 40 And if someone wants to sue you and take your tunic, let him have your cloak as well. 41 If someone forces you to go one mile, go with him two miles. 42 Give to

the one who asks you, and do not turn away from the one who wants to borrow from you.

[43] "You have heard that it was said, 'Love your neighbor and hate your enemy.' [44] But I tell you: Love your enemies and pray for those who persecute you, [45] that you may be sons of your Father in heaven. He causes his sun to rise on the evil and the good, and sends rain on the righteous and the unrighteous. [46] If you love those who love you, what reward will you get? Are not even the tax collectors doing that? [47] And if you greet only your brothers, what are you doing more than others? Do not even pagans do that? [48] Be perfect, therefore, as your heavenly Father is perfect.

A Radical Reading of Scripture (5:17–20)

Jesus made it clear he came to fulfill the Law, not destroy or abolish it. "The Law" or "the Prophets" referred to the Hebrew Scriptures. The Law held preeminence in the Jewish faith. It was central to Jewish life, and reading it was a primary event in the synagogue. The Law regulated Jewish practice and life. Jesus did not contradict the Law; he was determined to bring it to its intended goal—a covenant relationship with God.

The readers of the Law could not correctly interpret it until they understood how the Law was fulfilled in Jesus. The word "fulfill" in verse 17 means, "to fill out or expand." In other words, Jesus' life and ministry gave fuller meaning and understanding to God's laws. Each Old Testament Law must be interpreted in light of Jesus' life, purpose, and ministry. Jesus, the creator of the Law, both demonstrated and taught the people its true meaning and intent.

In verse 18, Jesus reaffirmed the authority of Scripture down to the smallest component of Hebrew words. The phrase "for truly" is translated as "amen." You have probably heard people in a congregation say "Amen" with this sense in mind. However, Jesus used this term before he spoke important truths, giving intense emphasis to the words that followed. Not one component of one word from God would cease to be authoritative.

People viewed heaven as a part of the physical universe, and when the word "heaven" was combined with the word "earth" in verse 18, the phrase represented the totality of creation. Jesus stated this to stress obedience to the Law is always required, and disobedience always results in negative consequences.

The smallest letter in the Hebrew alphabet is a jot, and a tittle is the least stroke of a pen; it resembles a bend or point similar to an apostrophe. This mark was used to distinguish between Hebrew words that look similar. In referring to these characters in the language, Jesus was emphasizing that merely affirming the Law is not enough. The Law of God must be practiced. Everyone must obey—not just those considered religious or righteous. God's people must commit to following the complete will of God by living according to the entire Law.

Matthew frequently paired together the scribes and Pharisees as objects of criticism, as he did in verse 19. Jesus made a bold statement that a true believer in God must have a greater righteousness than those two groups of people. In other words, the Pharisaic way of interpreting and living out the Law was incorrect and incomplete. To the Jew, no one was more righteous than a teacher of the Law. A rabbi's job included studying and knowing every aspect of the Law. According to Jesus, a time was coming (and had already arrived) in which God required more than strict legal correctness to be in

Divorce

The Book of Genesis does not include a clause regarding divorce. The Law did contain a restriction regarding divorce. It allowed a husband to divorce his wife if she acted indecently. The husband could give his wife a certificate of divorce and consider the issue settled. If the divorced woman married another man, and that second husband died or rejected her, she was not permitted to remarry her first husband.

In the New Testament, Mark recorded Jesus' teaching that divorce should not be encouraged. Matthew also recorded Jesus' teaching, specifying the clause in the Law regarding adultery or infidelity. Divorcing for other reasons, such as growing apart or financial disagreements, goes against God's design for marriage.

Relational Guidance

Jesus equated uncontrolled anger at another person with murder. Here are five guidelines for avoiding uncontrolled anger in our relationships:

1. Don't give unwanted advice.
2. Choose your battles carefully.
3. Evaluate the intensity of your feelings before sharing them.
4. State your feelings honestly.
5. Refrain from harsh or critical comments.

right relationship with God. People must follow Jesus in discipleship as a result of their repentance and trust in him.

Anger and Murder (5:21–26)

In verses 21–22, Jesus referred to the sixth commandment, "You shall not murder." Jesus did not replace the command but rather showed that a right understanding of the Law changes the way a person lived it out. Jesus connected anger to murder, emphasizing the importance of people loving one another instead of harboring wrongful anger. Anger has a proper place in rallying against sin and injustice. Not all anger is sinful. Jesus did not say anger and murder are equally sinful and worthy of equal punishment. However, human anger is rarely free from mixed motives like revenge. Wrongful anger can lead to a literal murder. It can also be expressed in harmful and cutting words that kill a person's spirit. In verse 22, the type of anger Jesus referenced was a deep anger, a malice that comes from the heart.

The exact meaning of the word *Raca* is unclear, but most likely it meant "empty-headed." It was an angry expression of contempt. To use this word was considered a legal matter and the offender could stand before a ruling council called the Sanhedrin. Jesus said those who call someone a "fool" are guilty of sin, and the punishment was the fire of hell. Jesus used the term *Gehenna*, which referred to a horrible place in the southern valley outside Jerusalem. In Old Testament times followers of Molech slaughtered children there, and the place was considered the city garbage dump where fires constantly burned. These intense punishments enforced Jesus's teaching that to hate someone is the same as committing murder in your heart.

Jesus made his point with two illustrations. The first involved a person making an animal sacrifice at the altar of the temple in Jerusalem. In this situation, the one making a sacrifice is guilty of making another person angry. Jesus instructed the person to leave their gift of worship at the altar and go make the relationship right again. Without reconciliation, the act of worship would be adversely affected. In the second illustration, Jesus referred to two litigants settling a matter out of court. He stated this should be done quickly because once the litigants reached the court it would be too late to reconcile. Not settling the issue quickly out of court could result in drastic consequences.

These two illustrations highlight the fact that anger affects a person's relationship not only with other people, but also with God. Therefore, Jesus urged his listeners to settle matters quickly and in person whenever possible. It is easier and more beneficial to settle the differences quickly, with the purpose of reconciliation. A person filled with sinful anger must reconcile with the other person and confess it to God as sin in order to worship in truth.

3-18-18

Lust and Adultery (5:27–30)

Jesus also spoke to the law of sexual purity. God designed sex to be a powerful blessing between a married man and woman. Adultery is damaging to marriage and is the culmination of lust and selfishness. Jesus taught that the act of adultery begins with a desire of the heart. Although lusting with the eyes and the act of adultery are not the same, they are equally damaging in a spiritual sense. Jesus referred to a look that is more than recognition of a beautiful person; it is a look with thoughts of impurity. Jesus showed the severity of sexual lust when he said it would be better to lose an eye or hand than to give in to lust. The eye and the hand are both involved in adultery. Unfaithfulness starts with a look, and if not stopped, the look will soon lead to a touch that can lead to adultery. Removing the eye or hand would not fix the problem of the heart. However, discipline of the eyes and hands is required to overcome lust. In other words, overcoming lust requires spiritual surgery rather than physical surgery.

Same word used for last supper (Lust) strong desire

Marriage and Divorce (5:31–32)

Adultery often leads to divorce. Jesus pointed to the Old Testament Law regarding divorce (Deuteronomy 24:1–4). Then he took it a step further. Grounds for divorce in the Law were a hot topic among the Pharisees in Jesus' day. One school of thought allowed a man to divorce his wife for any reason. The other line of thinking allowed divorce only in the case of adultery. Jewish law required divorce in the case of adultery. In this instance, a man could give his wife a certificate of divorce and release her from the marriage. Divorce was a legal matter that required a formal process and witnesses. This process prevented hasty divorces in the heat of the moment.

Jesus encouraged people to honor the sanctity of marriage and spoke against those who considered marriage disposable. His purpose was to focus on conduct, not on giving new laws regarding divorce. Moses did not command divorce, but he allowed it. God did not design marriage to be a contract that could be easily broken when one or both spouses found it inconvenient. Marriage is a covenantal relationship that requires continual faithfulness on the part of both husband and wife. Marriage is a relationship that should only be broken by physical death or sexual sin.

Vows and Promises (5:33–37)

An oath in the Old Testament was considered a serious promise to God. Oaths or vows were not required. In fact, Jesus discouraged his listeners from making them. However, if a person made a vow, it should be kept. The Pharisees avoided making an oath in the name of God by swearing by Jerusalem, heaven, earth, or something else. All of these belong to God, so by swearing by them a person was essentially swearing by the name of God. To put the focus back on the intention of the law, Jesus instructed his followers to make their words trustworthy. An honest person with good character did not need to take a vow to make their statements believable. Trustworthy words depend on character; vows cannot overcome a lack of character.

Revenge and Forgiveness (5:38–42)

Jesus directed this portion of his sermon to individuals who offended one another, not nations who were in conflict. His words had nothing to do with nations at war with each other. The original Law protected people from paying a price greater than the offense warranted. The goal of the Law, found in Exodus 21:23–25, was to prevent people from taking revenge. Once again in these verses, Jesus replaced the letter of the law with a focus on its deeper meaning. A follower of Jesus must be willing to suffer loss rather than make someone else suffer. This included physical suffering as well as loss of property. If a person slapped a Christian in the face, the Christian should walk away so not to engage in a fight. A practice in Roman culture allowed a soldier to demand that a citizen carry his gear and weapons for one mile to give the soldier a break. Jesus instructed his followers to go above and beyond what was normally accepted in society in order to demonstrate generosity and the Christian spirit.

Insult vs. Defending yourself

Neighbors and Enemies (5:43–48)

Jesus told his disciples to love even their enemies. If they loved only their neighbor, they were no different than the tax collectors (people without a relationship with God). People hated tax collectors because they took advantage of people and worked for the ruling government. One true sign of a follower of Jesus is an ability to love people who are against them or who persecute them. The word for "love" used in this instance referred to a generous and costly sacrifice for the good of another person. Those who love and greet their enemies show they are growing more like their heavenly Father. Jesus challenged his followers to be "perfect "which means "mature or whole." Perfection is unattainable, but the biblical concept of godliness is attainable. Loving even those who cause us harm is a sign of maturing godliness.

Live It Out

The Law cannot save us, but it can point out our shortcomings. Jesus showed people what the Law of God meant in its truest essence. It is not enough to obey the letter of the Law; Christians must also understand and obey its intentions. For example, does a man consider it adultery to look at a woman with lustful thoughts? Society encourages such behavior. Jesus condemns it. Jesus wants believers to live by a higher standard—himself. Living according to Jesus' teachings takes obedience and commitment. Commitment to following God's laws goes beyond our natural tendencies. We must rely on the power of the Holy Spirit and spiritual discipline in order to live according to God's ways. We cannot do it alone.

Questions

1. After reading Jesus' explanation of God's laws, how do you feel about your obedience to God?

2. Who are some "enemies" you need to love rather than despise?

3. Do others see you as a person whose "yes means yes" and "no means no?" Why or why not?

4. After reading Jesus' teaching on murder, how might you need to repent of anger?

5. What did Jesus mean when he told us to "be perfect as our heavenly Father is perfect?"

lesson 6

Kingdom Attitudes about Wealth and Worry

MAIN IDEA

Kingdom citizens should focus on making eternal investments, trusting God to meet their needs.

QUESTION TO EXPLORE

How can we make eternal investments while trusting God to meet our needs?

STUDY AIM

To choose to make eternal investments while trusting God to meet my needs

QUICK READ

Jesus taught on the importance of focusing on things of eternal value. Investing in eternal things can eliminate worry in this life.

DISCOVER
BELIEVE
LIVE
BIBLE STUDY GUIDE

Introduction

Here are some well-known thoughts about worry:

- Worry is like a treadmill. It gives you something to do, but it does not get you anywhere.
- Don't worry about your life. You are not going to survive it anyway.
- Women always worry about what men will forget. Men always worry about what women will remember.
- Worry is wasting today's time cluttering up tomorrow's opportunities with yesterday's troubles.
- A day of worry is more exhausting than a day of work.
- Don't worry; be happy!

Worry is a common malady in today's culture. Financial distress, family cohesiveness, the safety of service members overseas, the well-being of children at school can all cause even the calmest person to become anxious. Although worry is commonplace today, it is not new. Jesus addressed the issue in the Sermon on the Mount, the focal passage for this lesson. His admonitions are as applicable for the American population as they were for the people in Israel who heard this message first-hand.

Matthew 6:19–34

[19] "Do not store up for yourselves treasures on earth, where moth and rust destroy, and where thieves break in and steal. [20] But store up for yourselves treasures in heaven, where moth and rust do not destroy, and where thieves do not break in and steal. [21] For where your treasure is, there your heart will be also.

[22] "The eye is the lamp of the body. If your eyes are good, your whole body will be full of light. [23] But if your eyes are bad, your whole body will be full of darkness. If then the light within you is darkness, how great is that darkness!

[24] "No one can serve two masters. Either he will hate the one and love the other, or he will be devoted to the one and despise the other. You cannot serve both God and Money.

25 "Therefore I tell you, do not worry about your life, what you will eat or drink; or about your body, what you will wear. Is not life more important than food, and the body more important than clothes? 26 Look at the birds of the air; they do not sow or reap or store away in barns, and yet your heavenly Father feeds them. Are you not much more valuable than they? 27 Who of you by worrying can add a single hour to his life ?

28 "And why do you worry about clothes? See how the lilies of the field grow. They do not labor or spin. 29 Yet I tell you that not even Solomon in all his splendor was dressed like one of these. 30 If that is how God clothes the grass of the field, which is here today and tomorrow is thrown into the fire, will he not much more clothe you, O you of little faith? 31 So do not worry, saying, 'What shall we eat?' or 'What shall we drink?' or 'What shall we wear?' 32 For the pagans run after all these things, and your heavenly Father knows that you need them. 33 But seek first his kingdom and his righteousness, and all these things will be given to you as well. 34 Therefore do not worry about tomorrow, for tomorrow will worry about itself. Each day has enough trouble of its own.

Invest in Heavenly Treasures (6:19–21)

It is easy to separate the spiritual life from everyday living. Jesus showed how the two realms are interconnected. The Pharisees used religion to make money. Jesus taught his followers to have a healthy perspective on possessions. Materialism can easily enslave a person, but a person controlled by the Spirit can use material things for God's glory. Jesus urged his followers to focus on heaven, not on their existence on earth. Treasures in this lifetime are only temporary and typically only serve the owner. Treasures stored in heaven are endless and can be gained by serving others.

In ancient times, much of the wealth consisted of precious metals and cloth. In the hot and sandy climate of Palestine, moths and rust were common. Moths were a destructive force to cloth, and thieves could steal precious metals. Most of the homes were made of mud brick, which made them susceptible to break in. The Greek word for "break" literally means "break through." Thieves in that day could easily break through walls to rob a home.

Jesus did not say it was impossible for rich people to become Christians; he said wealth brought its own struggles. The rich spend a lot of time and energy protecting their assets, and even when they successfully keep those possessions, they cannot take their earthly treasures to heaven. Christians can avoid these dangers by sharing their possessions generously. Christians should not focus on the temporary financial rewards on earth, but rather on eternal rewards that please the Father.

"Heavenly treasure" is a broad term. These treasures cannot be stored in boxes and barns but are designed to be stored in heaven prior to one's arrival. These are things like character, integrity, obedience, sharing Christ with others, spiritual disciplines, and faith. Christians should use earthly wealth and resources to help others; good deeds cannot be destroyed. Our affections are naturally drawn to what we consider valuable. Generosity and compassion towards others are valuable commodities.

Focus Your Eyes (6:22–23)

Jesus used the eye to represent the attitude of the mind. If the eye is working properly, a person can see properly and the whole body functions properly. If the eye is not functioning properly, the entire body suffers. Therefore, an eye or mind focused on the things of God is illuminated; an eye focused on the things of the world does not let light through and is misguided regarding the truth. This results in a darkened and misdirected mind. As the saying goes, "outlook determines outcome."

Make a Choice (6:24)

Some translations use the word "mammon" in place of the word "money" in this passage. Mammon is an Aramaic term for wealth or property. Jesus used the imagery of a slave to make his point. A slave could not solely belong to two masters. However, it was common for owners to have co-ownership of a slave. In the Greco-Roman world, the types of slaves varied. It was possible

Seeing Clearly

Ancient biblical writings took a different view of the human eye than that of modern-day science. Science today has proven the eye is a receptive organ that allows light into the brain through the outside. In biblical times, people believed the eye transmitted light to the object in view. This is the understanding under which Jesus referred to the eye as a lamp of the body. Religious scholars of his day believed God enlightened one's eyes and connected the eyes with the understanding heart. Eyes that were "closed" or "darkened" lacked understanding. Ideally a person had eyes that were bright and open, which meant the person had knowledge and insight into the truth. Even a blind person could have spiritual eyes open to the truth. The Old Testament referred to God's eyes as all-seeing. In contrast, idols had eyes but they could not see.

for a slave to endear himself to an owner. In the case of two owners, the owner who showed dignity and affection to the slave would get more than his fair share of the slave's work.

Likewise, a slave of money will pretend to obey God but will obey money. If a person pursues riches, that person will pay a great price. However, if God grants riches, and those riches are used for God's glory, they will be a blessing rather than a burden.

What Kingdom are You Seeking? (6:25–34)

Jesus discussed the result of solely seeking material possessions. The result is worry. Jesus used the word "worry" six times in these verses, highlighting the results of focusing one's eyes on the wrong prize. Possessions will not meet all the needs of a person's life. The answers to spiritual questions will not be found in material things. Materialism promises fulfillment, but in reality, it only leaves a person wanting more. Riches can create more problems than they solve. Wrongly pursued, they can create a false sense of security, greed, or competition; and can end in tragedy.

Jesus did not warn against planning for the future; but he did warn against being anxious about the future. He used the basic needs for food

How to Halt Worry

Here are some steps to stop worry in your life:

1. As a reminder, write down specific instances when God has met your needs. Express your gratitude to him.
2. Talk honestly with God about your worries (1 Peter 5:7).
3. Seek to serve someone who is in need.
4. Take time to exercise (a great way to relieve stress.)
5. Keep a prayer journal.
6. Invest time in your relationships with friends and family members.

and clothing to highlight his message. Jesus was speaking to people who did not have a lot of material possessions, but they could relate to the need for food and clothing. He pointed out that when a person commits to God instead of money, God promises to provide for the needs of that person.

Jesus told the crowd to stop worrying. He did not suggest that a Christian wait idly by for God to provide for one's daily needs; he suggested that a Christian not worry as he or she takes responsibility for obtaining God's provisions. Christians should labor and maintain a good work ethic, but still rely on God to provide their jobs and the ability to perform those jobs. Jesus used the example of birds and how they obtain food. Birds rely on nature for their food; they do not need to worry about having enough. Humans have more opportunity than birds to utilize nature as a source of food.

Jesus also directed his listener's attention to the flowers of the field, most likely wild flowers, to focus on God's provision for clothing. The word "see" in verse 28 is better translated "learn from." Flowers and plants do less than birds to provide for their needs. God adorns both birds and vegetation with beauty and majesty that surpasses anything people can manufacture.

Jesus used the Jewish communication technique of taking one's mind from the lesser (plants and animals) to the greater (people). If God takes such care of animals and vegetation (that do not have as high a value as humans), how much more will he provide for those made in his own image?

Based on Jesus' argument, worry comes from a lack of trust in God and his goodness. In a strong sense, worry could be likened to practical atheism.

It is easy to mask worry by referring to it as a concern or a burden, but the results are the same. Worry is a destructive sin. The Greek word for worry means, "to be drawn in different directions." In other words, worry pulls people apart. By worrying that God will not provide the things necessary for a meaningful and fulfilling existence, people may shorten their lifespan. Nature depends on God for life, yet humans are pulled apart when they depend on themselves to sustain life.

In verse 31, Jesus posed three questions any person might ask. However, he makes the distinction that these questions are understandable for a person who does not know God, but they are inappropriate for a child of God to ask. God knows his children and he knows what they need. Therefore, there is no need for worry.

Verse 33 is a familiar verse and a popular chorus sung in churches. Disciples of Jesus should seek the things of God. They seek God's kingdom before seeking their personal desires or the things they need. The word "first" in this verse refers to a person's priority, not the first in order of time. Therefore, Christians should use their best effort to pursue God's kingdom and his righteousness. The key for a disciple is to seek God's will.

Seeking God's righteousness means seeking a right standing before God made possible by Jesus' death and resurrection. It is a righteousness that comes from God; it is not achieved by human effort. This passage has both present and future implications. A Christian should obey the will of God now as well as anticipate the coming of God's kingdom. Worrying about earthly things is the opposite of pursuing righteousness in God's kingdom.

Jesus also told his followers not to worry about tomorrow. The key to fulfilling this verse is to trust in God. A person who trusts in God does not need to worry about today or tomorrow. Tomorrow never comes; it is always today. If a person focuses only on today, it is easier to fight anxiety. Each day has trouble and Christians are not exempt from that trouble. However, a Christian can face the troubles of the world with faith in God, while those who do not trust in God face these same troubles with anxiety.

Live It Out

There is nothing wrong with making financial or material investments. Jesus did not speak against using our resources wisely to better our lives. He did speak against attitudes of greed and selfishness. Have you ever prayed and asked God to show you how you can use your resources to bless the lives of other people? Most of the wealthiest Christians I know have a giving spirit. They love to give to bless others. They share what God gives them, and it makes them happy.

We may not all be able to invest large sums of money, but we can all invest in eternal things. Sharing your faith, using your resources and gifts to bless your church and others, sharing your talents and abilities, and treating others with respect are all ways to make an eternal investment. The key is motive. If we invest only to get something back in return or to be recognized, our reward will be small and temporary. If we give because God has blessed us and we want to make a difference in the lives of others, our rewards will be significant and eternal.

Questions

1. What eternal investments have you made lately?

2. Who has invested in your life? How?

3. How have you been a slave to money in the past? What did you learn?

4. Go outside and look at the flowers and the birds. What thoughts do they raise in your mind about God's provision for them and for you?

5. What are some ways we can alleviate worry?

6. What are some of the negative ways worry affects us?

lesson 7

Discernment in the Kingdom

MAIN IDEA

Life in God's kingdom requires spiritual discernment.

QUESTION TO EXPLORE

How can we make wise spiritual decisions?

STUDY AIM

To evaluate the wisdom of my spiritual decisions

QUICK READ

Jesus told his listeners the importance of each Christian examining his or her life to make sure there are no obstacles to following him as he emphasized the need for spiritual discernment.

Introduction

The TV show *Total Blackout* was a thirty-minute reality program during which contestants had to compete against each other in total darkness. It first aired in 2012 and only lasted two seasons. It was a frustrating show to watch because total darkness makes even simple tasks difficult. Ever stumble in the dark and stub your toe? Ouch!

Sometimes discernment can feel like walking in the dark, but it is a daily part of our lives. We constantly make decisions based on what we can see or what we can know about specific people or situations. It is easier to make the right decisions when we can see things plainly, as they truly are in the light of day. The same is true spiritually. God promises to give us direction, but we must make sure we are not trying to follow him in the dark. Spiritual discernment requires clear eyes and a full heart.

Matthew 7:1–27

1 "Do not judge, or you too will be judged. 2 For in the same way you judge others, you will be judged, and with the measure you use, it will be measured to you.

3 "Why do you look at the speck of sawdust in your brother's eye and pay no attention to the plank in your own eye? 4 How can you say to your brother, 'Let me take the speck out of your eye,' when all the time there is a plank in your own eye? 5 You hypocrite, first take the plank out of your own eye, and then you will see clearly to remove the speck from your brother's eye.

6 "Do not give dogs what is sacred; do not throw your pearls to pigs. If you do, they may trample them under their feet, and then turn and tear you to pieces.

7 "Ask and it will be given to you; seek and you will find; knock and the door will be opened to you. 8 For everyone who asks receives; he who seeks finds; and to him who knocks, the door will be opened.

9 "Which of you, if his son asks for bread, will give him a stone? 10 Or if he asks for a fish, will give him a snake? 11 If you, then, though you are evil, know how to give good gifts to your children, how much more will your Father in heaven give good gifts to those who ask him! 12 So

in everything, do to others what you would have them do to you, for this sums up the Law and the Prophets.

13 "Enter through the narrow gate. For wide is the gate and broad is the road that leads to destruction, and many enter through it. 14 But small is the gate and narrow the road that leads to life, and only a few find it.

15 "Watch out for false prophets. They come to you in sheep's clothing, but inwardly they are ferocious wolves. 16 By their fruit you will recognize them. Do people pick grapes from thornbushes, or figs from thistles? 17 Likewise every good tree bears good fruit, but a bad tree bears bad fruit. 18 A good tree cannot bear bad fruit, and a bad tree cannot bear good fruit. 19 Every tree that does not bear good fruit is cut down and thrown into the fire. 20 Thus, by their fruit you will recognize them.

21 "Not everyone who says to me, 'Lord, Lord,' will enter the kingdom of heaven, but only he who does the will of my Father who is in heaven. 22 Many will say to me on that day, 'Lord, Lord, did we not prophesy in your name, and in your name drive out demons and perform many miracles?' 23 Then I will tell them plainly, 'I never knew you. Away from me, you evildoers!'

24 "Therefore everyone who hears these words of mine and puts them into practice is like a wise man who built his house on the rock. 25 The rain came down, the streams rose, and the winds blew and beat against that house; yet it did not fall, because it had its foundation on the rock. 26 But everyone who hears these words of mine and does not put them into practice is like a foolish man who built his house on sand. 27 The rain came down, the streams rose, and the winds blew and beat against that house, and it fell with a great crash."

Can We Judge? (7:1–6)

Jesus used a word for "judge" that can mean two different things: to analyze or evaluate; or to avenge or condemn. Christians are to discern right and wrong actions—to analyze or evaluate but not condemn. Only God has the right to judge in that fashion. Christians look into and assess each other's lives to encourage one another in the faith. However, this must be done without a judgmental or condemning attitude. In a difficult situation where a brother or sister has sinned, a Christian should seek to restore that person in love with a desire to help, not condemn. Others may treat us the way we treat them. The type of judgment and the measure of judgment by which we treat others will be returned to us—either by God or by others.

Jesus shared a hyperbole about a speck and a plank in an eye to illustrate his point, highlighting moral failures. How can a Christian judge another person when he has so many sins of his own? This is hypocrisy, especially when Christians judge others Christians whom God has forgiven. Jesus did not exempt Christians from holding each another accountable. Rather, Jesus instructed his followers to take care of confessing and *repenting of their own sin first*, and then they could see clearly to help another Christian who has erred. The purpose behind such a confrontation is healing and restoration, not judgment and shame.

God entrusts his people with holy things. Jesus used wild, ravaging dogs and unclean pigs as metaphors to allude to people who reject the gospel and aggressively oppose it. The gospel should be preached to all people; however, some people will reject the truth. Jesus warned against spending too much time and effort on those who have obviously hardened their hearts toward him. For example, Jesus refused to talk to Herod about his identity and Paul refused to argue with people who resisted his message. It is OK to move on after a person repeatedly rejects the gospel, because continuing to push the issue with some people would be counterproductive.

Ask, Seek, and Knock (7:7–12)

Interestingly Jesus turned his focus to prayer, connecting it with discernment. God alone judges perfectly, so his followers should ask for discernment constantly. Believers make mistakes and therefore must ask for wisdom and direction. Jesus encouraged his readers to pray with an expectant attitude, telling them to ask, seek, and knock. The use of the three-word approach added emphasis to his statement and promoted persistence in prayer. A believer who continues to ask will continue to receive, the one who continues to seek will continue to find, and the one who continues to knock on the door will continue to see doors open up.

The emphasis in this section is on the faithfulness of the Father to grant his children's request, not on the person's ability to impress God with his requests. Jesus compared God the Father and earthly fathers with a series of rhetorical questions, all of which would be answered with "no." Jesus sought to change the image of God as an angry judge to that of a loving father. If sinful fathers know how to give good gifts to their children, how much more would the perfect Father (God) desire to give good things to his children? Even evil parents know how to give good gifts. How much more would a perfect, holy, and good God know how to give to his children? Again Jesus used the lesser-to-greater argument to make his point, with human parents being the lesser, and God the Father being the greater. God provides for the needs of his children and loves his children more than their human parents can love them.

Jesus provided a guiding principle to direct the thoughts and actions of his followers as they encounter other people. This principle is often called the Golden Rule, and it guards believers against being critical of others and prideful of one's spiritual status. Jesus used the phrase in a positive manner—treat others in the manner you would like to be treated. Jesus used it to highlight the importance of serving others. Verse 12 sums up the lessons of the first 11 verses of this chapter.

Narrow and Wide Gates (7:13–14)

False teachers existed in Jesus' day, and they still exist today. They are dangerous and deceptive, but the greatest danger is self-deception. Jesus used two images to help a person recognize the right choice: the image of a gate and the image of a road. The narrow gate represents the decision to follow Jesus, while the wide gate is a sinful life that defies God. A narrow gate is not easily noticed, just as the choice to follow Jesus is not always obvious. Living life by following Jesus' teachings is like squeezing through a small opening that is sharply defined. Entry through this gate also requires going against one's natural inclinations to follow the crowd and avoid making a tough choice.

In verse 14 Jesus referred to the narrow road. The entry point of knowing God is narrow—through the person and work of Christ. The continual road of following him remains narrow. His listeners would readily understand the image of a narrow passageway between high rocks. Following Jesus requires giving up the things of the world that would make it impossible to pass through the narrow space between the rocks. Earlier, Jesus had stated his followers cannot serve two masters; neither can they walk on two roads simultaneously. You can choose the wide road (the most popular, well-traveled road of disobedience), or you can choose the narrow road, a life of faith in Christ.

True and False Prophets and Disciples (7:15–23)

Jesus compared false teachers to wolves and bad trees. A true prophet spoke directly from God. Prophets could help a person find the narrow road, or they could lead people down the wide road to destruction. In first-century Israel, people respected prophets and their authority. Many false prophets tried to speak with authority from God. These false teachers easily swayed people to follow their teachings rather than scriptural truth. The false teachers looked as innocent as sheep, but they were actually ravenous wolves with appetites to deceive people for personal profit.

Therefore, it is vital for Christians to discern true from false prophets. This could be done by examining a prophet's actions and the fruit of his life. Jesus warned his listeners to watch what a prophet does before being influenced by his words. Jesus made the point that a bad tree cannot produce good fruit, just as a false teacher cannot teach what is true. Even though a false prophet's behavior may disguise his evil intent, his teachings will reveal his true nature.

Jesus shared the fate of false teachers by comparing them to what happens to a tree that does not bear good fruit. The bad tree is cut down and removed to make room for good trees. The owner then burns down the diseased tree to prevent it from spreading bad seeds. Such is the future of false teachers.

Jesus then spoke about those who follow him as disciples. As in the case of the false teachers, a believer's life reveals whether or not he truly follows Christ. Although only God knows a person's actual spiritual state, others can look for evidence that a person's life matches his words. Jesus made it

Prophets

Prophets existed in both the Old and New Testaments. The Old Testament word for prophet meant "spokesman" or "speaker." A prophet was a person authorized to speak for God. Moses was one such Old Testament prophet. Later on, criteria were established to prove a prophet's authenticity. For example, a prophet had to be an Israelite who spoke in the name of the Lord. In addition, their predictions had to come true, and their message had to be in line with the written revelation of God (the Bible). If a prophet failed any of these tests, he was considered a pseudo or false prophet.

The role of the prophet in the New Testament was similar. They were people moved by the Holy Spirit to deliver special messages from God to his people. God gifted them for that task. Many modern scholars believe that with the completion of the Bible, prophetic words and the gift of prophecy ceased to exist. They believe that the Holy Spirit now guides people without the help of prophets.

clear that simply saying, "Lord, Lord" was not enough to gain entrance into the kingdom of heaven. Words and religious activities are not substitutes for obedience. The fact Jesus will say to some people he never knew them reveals they were never a part of Christ in the first place.

Jesus was not speaking about people who were once believers but lost their salvation, because the Bible teaches that our salvation rests on what Jesus did on the cross. However, a person can do "Christian things" without being a Christian. Hearing God's word must result in doing God's word. Prophecy, driving out demons, and miracles are divine activities, but they are no substitute for repentance and allegiance to Christ. Obedience is evidence of true faith.

Wise and Foolish Builders (7:24–27)

Jesus claimed to have the same authority as God the Father. He set obedience to his teachings over and above the self-righteous acts of the Pharisees. He used a comparison again, this time using builders and buildings to make

Identifying False Teachers

Here are some questions to ask that can help to identify false teachers:

1. Do they teach anything contrary to the Bible?
2. Do they encourage you to study the Bible on your own?
3. Do you feel uneasiness when you hear them teach, like something being said is not quite accurate or truthful?
4. What is the main subject of their messages?
5. Do they preach another gospel than that of salvation through faith alone in Jesus Christ?

his point. The two builders in the story have much in common. Both built a house. Both houses looked good and were well-built. The storm (which represents God's judgment) blew against both houses, and only the house built on the solid foundation withstood the high winds and rain.

In the same way, people can look alike and have the same desires, but only those who build their lives on a true faith in Christ will survive the judgment. Although lives can look the same, only the life built on a relationship with Christ will be left standing. Christ can withstand the daily storms, and especially the final storm of judgment. In times of crisis (like a storm), a person's faith is proven. Jesus concluded his argument as he proclaimed that every person much choose whether to accept or reject him.

Live It Out

Life experiences reveal whether or not a person is truly a follower of Christ. These tests usually come during times of difficulty or stress. The same test that reveals our faith can also be used to determine if someone else is a believer. Christ told believers not to judge others in regard to their salvation. However, he did say a person's belief (or lack thereof) would be revealed in his words and actions. The Holy Spirit will help us discern lies from the truth. Growing in our knowledge and understanding of God will help protect us from those who teach things contrary to the word of God.

Questions

1. How would someone else describe your faith in Christ? Are they able to see Christ in your actions?

2. What process do you follow when you have to make a tough decision or have to discern between right and wrong?

3. Who are some false teachers of our time, preachers or leaders who deceive people about what it means to follow Jesus?

4. How do you respond to accountability?

5. Think about a time when you felt judged by another person. How did it make you feel? What did you do about it?

6. Where do you draw the line between "not giving to dogs that which is sacred" and continuing to "ask, seek, and knock?" When is it OK to give up on someone you are trying to reach?

UNIT THREE

Parables of the Kingdom

Unit Three, "Parables of the Kingdom," consists of three lessons that concentrate on three of the parables King Jesus used to describe various aspects of his kingdom. Lesson eight focuses on the Parable of the Sower which reveals how the condition of our heart determines our response to Jesus and his word. Lesson nine discusses how the Parable of the Unmerciful Servant shows that kingdom citizens should extend forgiveness to others instead of "keeping score." Lesson ten uses the Parable of the Workers in the Vineyard to describe how membership in God's kingdom is granted through his generous grace and is available to all.

lesson 8

Seed Sowing and Secret Truths

MAIN IDEA

The condition of our hearts determines our response to Jesus and his word.

QUESTION TO EXPLORE

What is the current condition of my heart?

STUDY AIM

To assess the condition of my heart and its receptivity to God's word

QUICK READ

Jesus described the variety of ways in which people respond to the gospel, reminding us that although many will reject the gospel, some will embrace it.

DISCOVER
BIBLE
STUDY
GUIDE
BELIEVE
LIVE

Introduction

My family had just returned from a week in Pensacola, Florida where we once lived when I served as pastor of a church in that city. My wife Jan and I enjoyed seeing many of our friends and our children got to spend time with their old buddies. Our daughter Cara wanted to spend extra time with one of her close friends, so we picked her up and headed back to the beach.

Cara's friend was sometimes a little slow in catching on to things, and that had not changed since we left Pensacola. As we drove back to the beach, Cara read some jokes out of a book. After each joke, her friend would have a blank look on her face until Cara explained the joke; then the friend would laugh. Sometimes we all can be a little slow to catch on to things, whether they be jokes or some other concept or issue.

Jesus must have felt that way about his disciples at times. Jesus could understand why his enemies in the crowd did not comprehend his parables, because they had hardened their hearts against him. However, the lack of understanding displayed by his disciples often frustrated him. Such was the case in our text. Jesus presented a parable to the disciples and to the crowd, and then later explained its meaning to his disciples.

Matthew 13:1–23

1 That same day Jesus went out of the house and sat by the lake. 2 Such large crowds gathered around him that he got into a boat and sat in it, while all the people stood on the shore. 3 Then he told them many things in parables, saying: "A farmer went out to sow his seed. 4 As he was scattering the seed, some fell along the path, and the birds came and ate it up. 5 Some fell on rocky places, where it did not have much soil. It sprang up quickly, because the soil was shallow. 6 But when the sun came up, the plants were scorched, and they withered because they had no root. 7 Other seed fell among thorns, which grew up and choked the plants. 8 Still other seed fell on good soil, where it produced a crop—a hundred, sixty or thirty times what was sown. 9 He who has ears, let him hear."

10 The disciples came to him and asked, "Why do you speak to the people in parables?"

[11] He replied, "The knowledge of the secrets of the kingdom of heaven has been given to you, but not to them. [12] Whoever has will be given more, and he will have an abundance. Whoever does not have, even what he has will be taken from him. [13] This is why I speak to them in parables:

"Though seeing, they do not see;
   though hearing, they do not hear or understand.

[14] In them is fulfilled the prophecy of Isaiah: "'You will be ever hearing but never understanding; you will be ever seeing but never perceiving. [15] For this people's heart has become calloused; they hardly hear with their ears, and they have closed their eyes. Otherwise they might see with their eyes, hear with their ears, understand with their hearts and turn, and I would heal them.' [16] But blessed are your eyes because they see, and your ears because they hear. [17] For I tell you the truth, many prophets and righteous men longed to see what you see but did not see it, and to hear what you hear but did not hear it. [18] "Listen then to what the parable of the sower means: [19] When anyone hears the message about the kingdom and does not understand it, the evil one comes and snatches away what was sown in his heart. This is the seed sown along the path. [20] The one who received the seed that fell on rocky places is the man who hears the word and at once receives it with joy. [21] But since he has no root, he lasts only a short time. When trouble or persecution comes because of the word, he quickly falls away. [22] The one who received the seed that fell among the thorns is the man who hears the word, but the worries of this life and the deceitfulness of wealth choke it, making it unfruitful. [23] But the one who received the seed that fell on good soil is the man who hears the word and understands it. He produces a crop, yielding a hundred, sixty or thirty times what was sown."

The Parable of the Sower (13:1–9)

Our text opens with Jesus sitting by a lake (13:1). A large crowd soon surrounded him, transforming his place of meditation into a classroom. Jesus often taught during the regular synagogue service (see Mark 1:21) and later in the temple (John 18:20). However, he did not limit his teachings to the synagogue or the temple; he addressed crowds wherever they gathered. He spoke to the people in a mountain location (Matt. 5:1); while he was with them in a house (Mark 2:1); and even in a cemetery (John 11:38). Jesus reflected that same flexibility in our text when he used a boat as his pulpit (Matt. 13:2).

Matthew tells us Jesus "told them many things in parables" (13:3). Jesus often utilized parables as he taught the multitudes. The term "parable" covers a variety of literature types, including maxims, ethical sayings, moral illustrations, and even allegories. However, the term usually applies to stories that illustrate spiritual truths, like the story in our text. Jesus used these parables primarily to describe the kingdom of God.

Jesus painted a picture the people of first-century Palestine could easily recognize. The land was full of farmers, and one of the responsibilities of farmers was to sow the seed so they could later bring in the harvest. Jesus did not provide any details about the farmer himself. Was he old or young? Was he an experienced farmer? Was he conscientious in fulfilling his responsibilities? Jesus did not say. Instead, Jesus focused attention on the soil on which the seeds fell.

Jesus identified four specific kinds of soils upon which the seeds fell. He referred to the first soil as "the path." This seed did not produce results because

Parable

The word "parable" comes from two Greek words that mean, "to throw" and "alongside." Therefore, a parable is a story told to illustrate a truth. Jesus did not invent the parable, but he perfected the use of it in his teaching ministry. Jesus drew his parables from the familiar events of everyday life: a farmer sowing his seeds; a young son rebelling against his father; a person losing a coin; a mustard seed. Jesus' parables were also marked by the element of surprise: a forgiven servant who refused to forgive someone else; or a dishonest servant who drew the praise of his master; a man who humbly chose the worst seat at the banquet who was invited to sit instead in a seat of honor. Jesus used parables as windows through which his listeners could see glimpses of the kingdom of God. Parables also served as mirrors into which his followers looked to gain a better understanding of themselves.

"the birds came and ate it up" (13:4). The second soil Jesus called "rocky places." Rocks were prominent in first-century Palestine (and still are). One myth suggested God gave two angels the responsibility to scatter rocks across the earth, but when one of the angels was passing over Palestine, the sack broke, and all of the rocks fell out. A thin layer of soil covered the rocks, and the seed took root in that veneer of soil. Unable to establish their roots down into the soil, those plants immediately thrust upward, giving an initial expectation these seeds would produce a crop. However, the early promise quickly evaporated, because the plants "withered because they had no root" (13:5–6).

At first glance, the third soil—the ground that contained thorns—seemed more promising than the first two. At least this soil provided a place where the seed could send down its roots and erupt from the ground as a plant. Unfortunately, the thorns also sprang up out of this soil and ultimately "choked the plants" (13:7).

The fourth soil Jesus described differed from the other three because it was receptive to the seeds. In this soil, the seeds took root and no thorns choked out the fledgling plants. As a result, that seed "produced a crop—a hundred, sixty, or thirty times what was sown" (13:8). Rather than read special meaning into the different levels of harvest, we need to accept it as a reinforcement of the message of the parable. Even when the seed fell on the good soil, the response to the seed varied according to the condition of the good soil.

Jesus ended the parable with a phrase that often appears in the New Testament, seven times in the Gospels and eight times in Revelation: "He who has ears, let him hear." This statement places responsibility on the hearer. Individuals must choose how they will respond to the gospel. Jesus developed this thought in the verses that followed.

The Teaching Method (13:10–17)

The disciples asked Jesus to explain why he taught in parables (13:10). Jesus described the dual character of his parables: they enlighten and confound at the same time. To some, the parables reveal "the secrets of the kingdom of God" (13:11). These "secrets" are those things that a person cannot discern apart from God's revelation. Jesus affirmed that some people discerned these truths through his parables. Others listened to Jesus' parables but did not understand them. To them, the parables did not teach but rather baffled them. Why was this so? Jesus used Isaiah 6:9 to answer that question.

But what does this quote—or rather paraphrase—from Isaiah mean? Jesus explained that God gives to those who "have an abundance" but takes away from "whoever does not have" (13:12). God can only fill a glass that is already full. In other words, Jesus' disciples grasped the meaning of the parable because of something they already possessed, while many in the crowds did not grasp the meaning of the parable because of something they did not possess. That "something" was faith in him. Those who responded to the saving word of God through Jesus Christ could understand "the secrets of the kingdom of God," but those who failed to respond in faith could not discern the deeper meanings of Jesus' teaching. They simply did not have the spiritual "ears to hear."

Perhaps that is why Jesus used parables. The crowds still flocked after him, but did they understand what Jesus asked of them? And were they willing to pay the price? Perhaps he used parables to sort out those who genuinely believed in him from those who were drawn to the excitement his work generated.

The Explanation (13:18–23)

Beginning in verse 18, Jesus explained the meaning of the parable to the disciples. He did not identify the sower, but he did identify the seed as "the message about the kingdom" (13:19). Then he described different responses to this message, represented by the various kinds of soil in his parable. The "path" represented those who heard the word but could not comprehend it (13:19). The rocky soil represented those who embraced the word initially, but they did not stay once they realized the demands of receiving the word in a life-changing way (13:20–21). The soil that produced weeds described those who wanted to receive the word but allowed the "worries of this life and the deceitfulness of wealth" to choke it out (13:22). The good soil represented those who heard the word and accepted it. In their lives, the seed of the gospel took root, survived any threat posed by weeds, and produced a crop.

What are we to make of this parable? We need to be careful about extracting a theology of salvation from the elements of the story. For example, we should not try to conclude that the third soil suggested a person could have faith and then lose it. That is not the point of the parable. Nor should we use Jesus' reference to Isaiah as a justification for predestination, implying some will understand Jesus' words and respond to them, and that others cannot understand Jesus' words because God predetermined they would not. That interpretation goes far beyond the meaning of the text.

So what are we to make of this parable? To the crowds who followed him, Jesus warned that it was not enough just to hear his word. They must allow his word to take root in their hearts through a consistent faith so the seed could produce in their lives the fruit of righteousness. To the Twelve and to the women who followed him, Jesus was explaining a phenomenon they were observing. Some people accepted Jesus' word and followed him joyfully, while others rejected his word and were lining up against him. Why? The condition of their hearts determined their response to his word.

Live It Out

Jesus' parable presents a word of warning to the church today. As we plant the word of the gospel in the world, the response will not always be positive. Instead of being discouraged by such rejections of the message, we must simply accept the varying responses. Instead of being stopped by negative responses, we need to be motivated by them.

Receiving the Word

- We need to prepare our hearts in order to receive the word of the gospel.
- We need to deepen our faith in order to nurture the word of the gospel.
- We need to clean our lives in order to develop the word of the gospel.
- We need to enrich our hearts in order to multiply the fruit of the gospel.

Jesus' parable also provides a word of hope to the church. This is the other side of the coin. The response will not always be positive, but it *will* be positive some of the time. That is the good news illustrated in the fourth soil in Jesus' parable. The fourth soil is called "good soil." When the word of the gospel is planted in this soil, the result will be abundant fruit for the kingdom of God. It is important for the church to focus on that rather than any negative response to the gospel.

Questions

1. What causes some hearts to be open to the gospel and others to be closed to it?

2. What can the church do to nourish the soil before and during the time we share the seed of the gospel?

3. In what ways does Jesus' parable encourage us as we share the seed of the gospel? In what ways does it warn us?

4. How does Jesus' use of parables compare to the teaching and preaching done in your church?

5. How would you describe the soil of your heart? Why?

lesson 9

Forgiveness in the Kingdom

MAIN IDEA
Kingdom citizens extend forgiveness to others instead of "keeping score."

QUESTION TO EXPLORE
Do we "keep score" or extend forgiveness to others?

STUDY AIM
To accept the challenge to extend forgiveness to others instead of "keeping score"

QUICK READ
Jesus used a parable to illustrate the damage done when believers refuse to forgive each other in the same spirit by which God has forgiven them.

DISCOVER
BELIEVE
LIVE

BIBLE
STUDY
GUIDE

Introduction

In the fading days of the Roman Empire, Celtic tribesmen abducted a sixteen-year-old boy and sold him into slavery in Ireland, where he labored under the harshest conditions. After more than five years of this slave labor, he managed to escape. After walking two hundred miles to a seaport, he found passage on a ship that carried him back home to safety. However, once he returned home, he was plagued by dreams in which his captors begged him to come back to Ireland and share the word of Christ with them.

This young man pushed aside his fears and decided to respond to the request of these people who haunted his dreams. Instead of bearing a grudge against his captors, he left the safety of his homeland and returned to Ireland, the land of his captivity. He soon abandoned his English name, Patricius, and took up the name of Patrick. Because he was willing to forgive his captors and take the word of Christ to them, this young man eventually became the Patron Saint of Ireland, St. Patrick. Patrick demonstrated the kind of forgiveness Jesus called for in this text.

Matthew 18:21–35

21 Then Peter came to Jesus and asked, "Lord, how many times shall I forgive my brother when he sins against me? Up to seven times?"

22 Jesus answered, "I tell you, not seven times, but seventy-seven times.

23 "Therefore, the kingdom of heaven is like a king who wanted to settle accounts with his servants. 24 As he began the settlement, a man who owed him ten thousand talents was brought to him. 25 Since he was not able to pay, the master ordered that he and his wife and his children and all that he had be sold to repay the debt.

26 "The servant fell on his knees before him. 'Be patient with me,' he begged, 'and I will pay back everything.' 27 The servant's master took pity on him, canceled the debt and let him go.

28 "But when that servant went out, he found one of his fellow servants who owed him a hundred denarii. He grabbed him and began to choke him. 'Pay back what you owe me!' he demanded.

> ²⁹ "His fellow servant fell to his knees and begged him, 'Be patient with me, and I will pay you back.'
> ³⁰ "But he refused. Instead, he went off and had the man thrown into prison until he could pay the debt. ³¹ When the other servants saw what had happened, they were greatly distressed and went and told their master everything that had happened.
> ³² "Then the master called the servant in. 'You wicked servant,' he said, 'I canceled all that debt of yours because you begged me to. ³³ Shouldn't you have had mercy on your fellow servant just as I had on you?' ³⁴ In anger his master turned him over to the jailers to be tortured, until he should pay back all he owed.
> ³⁵ "This is how my heavenly Father will treat each of you unless you forgive your brother from your heart."

Peter's Question (18:21–22)

The word "then" reminds us that the text has a context. Peter raised this question about forgiveness in response to Jesus' explanation of how we should respond to someone who has sinned against us (18:15–17). Jesus' instruction on how we should forgive others fits into the larger context of Jesus' discussion of how believers should relate to each other (18:1–35). In the first section, Jesus urged his listeners not to act in such a way as to drive other disciples away; he described God's desire that not one of his people fall away (18:1–14). In the second section of this larger discussion, Jesus instructed his listeners to seek to restore individuals who have strayed from the fellowship of believers by offering them forgiveness (18:15–35). Jesus' description of the process for forgiving one another prompted Peter's question: "How many times shall I forgive my brother?" (18:21).

Peter probably thought he was being generous when he offered to forgive "up to seven times" because the Jewish rabbis limited forgiveness to three times. Peter's offer of forgiveness doubled the pattern recommended by the rabbis. However, instead of congratulating Peter for his generous gesture, Jesus shattered his smugness with a figure that conveys a different understanding of forgiveness altogether (18:22). In the NIV, Jesus recommended forgiving "seventy-seven times." In the NASB, Jesus suggested forgiving "seventy times seven times."

Whichever number is correct, trying to determine the exact number puts us in the same limiting mindset Peter demonstrated. Jesus used numbers that were considered "perfect" in his day: seven multiplied by ten. This implies forgiveness should be taken to an infinite degree. In other words, Jesus countered Peter's attempt to limit his forgiveness with the reminder that when believers begin counting the number of times they forgive, they have not really forgiven at all. Forgiveness is a state of mind, not a mathematical formula. Paul captured this truth in his Corinthian letter when he wrote that Christian love "keeps no record of wrongs" (1 Corinthians 13:5).

Jesus' Parable (18:23–34)

Jesus illustrated this spirit of forgiveness with a parable that only Matthew records. Notice Matthew used the term "kingdom of heaven" instead of the term "kingdom of God," which is used in the other Gospels (18:23). Both terms refer to the fellowship of believers. In the parable, Jesus did not address the question of how we can become a part of the kingdom of heaven, but rather how we should act once we become a part of it. He did not prescribe the attitude Christians are to have toward unbelievers, but rather how believers should treat each other.

Jesus' dramatic parable unfolds in three acts. In Act I, a king decided to settle accounts with his servants (18:23). Most commentators conclude that these "servants" were high officials in the kingdom who collected taxes from the citizens and had to give an account of that money. Of the many servants brought before the king, Jesus focused on one particular official who owed the king "ten thousand talents" (18:24).

Commentators attempt to calculate the exact amount of money represented by the "ten thousand talents." Whatever calculation they use, Jesus' point was clear: the official owed more to the king than he could earn in a lifetime, and thus he bore a debt he would never be able to pay. Jesus contrasted the king's initial response (18:25), which the official deserved, with his ultimate response (18:27), which the official did not deserve.

The king initially proposed the standard response to unpaid debt in the first-century world. The debtor, his family, and everything he owned would be sold to apply to the debt. When the official begged for mercy, the king altered his response. Instead of selling the man and his family into slavery and thus dooming them to ultimate destruction, the king decided to forgive the man's debt, thus offering him another chance. In this remarkable act of mercy, the king "canceled the debt and let him go" (18:27).

In Act II, the forgiven official left the king's presence only to confront another individual who owed him money (18:28). The size of this debt was miniscule when compared to the official's debt to the king. Some commentaries calculate the official's debt to the king at about ten million dollars in today's money, while this servant's debt to the official was not more than one hundred. Instead of forgiving this debt because he himself had been forgiven a stupendous debt, the official physically seized the servant and demanded he repay the debt immediately (18:29). When the servant begged for time to repay the debt, the official refused to grant forgiveness and instead had the servant thrown into jail (18:30). The official responded to his debtor with cruelty instead of compassion and with vengeance instead of forgiveness.

In Act III, the official's cruelty caught up with him. Witnesses to the man's poor treatment of his debtor recognized the incongruity of his actions, so they reported his action to the king (18:31). Appalled at the ingratitude of his

Forgive

The word translated "forgive" in this text is the Greek word *aphiemi*, which means "to leave" or "to leave behind." Matthew used the word to describe what James and John did when Jesus called them to be his disciples (Matthew 4:22). Matthew wrote, "they left [*aphiemi*] the boat and their father." In John 4:28, the word describes what the woman at the well in Samaria did after Jesus transformed her life. John wrote, "leaving [*aphiemi*] the water jar, the woman went back to the town." Both of these references picture someone walking away from something—from the boat and from the jar and well. Those pictures describe what it means to forgive. It means to walk away from something and leave it behind. As God walks away from our sin when he forgives it, we should walk away from the sin of others as we forgive them.

official, the king immediately brought back the first servant for another confrontation. At this point, the official had no chance to issue another request
for leniency. Instead, the king silenced whatever request he might have made
by condemning his action and accusing him of ingratitude (18:32–33). This
time, instead of forgiving his debt and setting him free, the king punished
the official and demanded he pay his debt in full (18:34)—a debt he could
never hope to repay.

Jesus' Warning (18:35)

As we read the concluding statement in Jesus' parable about forgiveness, we
need to remember Jesus' parable does not suggest God's likeness to a king,
but instead implies his distinction from a king. We see parallels to Jesus'
description of God here with a statement he tagged on to another of his
parables.

In Luke 11:1–13, Jesus described a person who approached his neighbor
at midnight and asked for some bread because an unexpected guest had
come to stay with him. Even though the man was inconvenienced, he got
out of bed and gave to his neighbor the requested loaves of bread. Jesus then
tagged onto this parable a description of how human fathers respond to the
requests of their children. If the child asks for a fish, the father will not offer
a snake. If the child wants an egg, the father will not contribute a scorpion.
Jesus followed this description of the actions of a human father with the
statement: "If you then, though you are evil, know how to give good gifts to

Case Study

You are the teacher of an adult Sunday school class that regularly communicates via email. A member of the class accidently includes you on
an email to another person in which he says some cruel and unkind
things about you. How should you respond? Should you confront the
person who made the unkind statements? Should you talk to the person
who received the email, making sure he does not fall into the same trap?
Or should you simply forget the email altogether?

your children, how much more will your Father in heaven give the Holy Spirit to those who ask him!" (Luke 11:13).

That "how much more" dynamic runs through this parable in Matthew 18, except this time Jesus contrasted God with a human king instead of with a human father. Jesus did not suggest God would follow the methods of a human king by torturing someone who has an unforgiving heart. Instead, Jesus affirmed if human kings expect their subjects to display forgiveness, how much more does our Heavenly King expect us to respond in that way?

Live It Out

The central point of Jesus' parable applies to believers today as much as it did to the first disciples. The willingness to forgive is the key to effectively doing the work of the kingdom. Unfortunately, hurt feelings and the thirst for revenge often neutralize our effectiveness. This was true in the first-century church. The bickering between the Greek and Hebrew widows in Acts 6:1, as well as the split between Paul and Barnabas in Acts 15:39–40, clearly illustrate this problem. It is also true today, as anyone involved in church work will quickly testify.

Running through the parable is another implication. We do not forgive others in order to get God to forgive us. Instead, we forgive others because God has already forgiven us. That attitude toward others results from being a part of the kingdom of God. Because we have been forgiven, we forgive others.

Questions

1. What is the problem with Peter's question about how many times he should forgive?

2. What do you think causes petty arguments in the church?

3. If you are in conflict with someone in your church, what steps can you take to bring about reconciliation?

4. Can you remember an incident in which the unwillingness of a person to forgive someone else detracted from the ministry of your church?

5. How have you witnessed extraordinary forgiveness in your church?

6. Whom do you need to forgive? Why have you withheld forgiveness?

lesson 10

Membership in the Kingdom

MAIN IDEA

Membership in God's kingdom is permitted through his generous grace and is available to all.

QUESTION TO EXPLORE

Do we prefer God's justice or his grace when it comes to including people in his kingdom?

STUDY AIM

To express thankfulness to God for his generous grace in including me in his kingdom

QUICK READ

When we calculate our blessings from God or compare our blessings to those of others, we will miss out on the gracious generosity of God.

DISCOVER
BELIEVE
LIVE
BIBLE STUDY GUIDE

Introduction

One of Jesus' best-known parables described two brothers, one who ran away from home and wasted his money in squanderous living while the other brother remained at home as a dutiful son (Luke 15). However, when the prodigal returned, the father welcomed him with a celebratory feast in which he killed the fatted calf and lavished his goodness on this son who had been found. The older brother protested that the father treated him unfairly because the father never had a celebratory feast for him. The father reminded the older son he had no reason to complain because he had been enjoying his father's blessings all along.

Jesus wove a similar theme through the parable in Matthew 20:1–16. In the previous chapter, the rich young ruler refused to make the sacrifice necessary to follow Jesus. This prompted Peter to raise the question, "What then will there be for us?" (19:27). Peter's question needed to be answered. Even more important, the attitude that motivated his question needed to be addressed. In the parable in this lesson, Jesus dealt with both the question and the questioner. In so doing, he shed light on the gracious generosity of God.

Matthew 20:1–16

[1] "For the kingdom of heaven is like a landowner who went out early in the morning to hire men to work in his vineyard. [2] He agreed to pay them a denarius for the day and sent them into his vineyard.

[3] "About the third hour he went out and saw others standing in the marketplace doing nothing. [4] He told them, 'You also go and work in my vineyard, and I will pay you whatever is right.' [5] So they went.

"He went out again about the sixth hour and the ninth hour and did the same thing. [6] About the eleventh hour he went out and found still others standing around. He asked them, 'Why have you been standing here all day long doing nothing?'

[7] "'Because no one has hired us,' they answered.

"He said to them, 'You also go and work in my vineyard.'

[8] "When evening came, the owner of the vineyard said to his foreman, 'Call the workers and pay them their wages, beginning with the last ones hired and going on to the first.'

> 9 "The workers who were hired about the eleventh hour came and each received a denarius. 10 So when those came who were hired first, they expected to receive more. But each one of them also received a denarius. 11 When they received it, they began to grumble against the landowner. 12 'These men who were hired last worked only one hour,' they said, 'and you have made them equal to us who have borne the burden of the work and the heat of the day.'
>
> 13 "But he answered one of them, 'Friend, I am not being unfair to you. Didn't you agree to work for a denarius? 14 Take your pay and go. I want to give the man who was hired last the same as I gave you. 15 Don't I have the right to do what I want with my own money? Or are you envious because I am generous?'
>
> 16 "So the last will be first, and the first will be last."

The Landowner's Call to Work (20:1–7)

Jesus told his listeners about a landowner who went out early in the morning to hire workers for his vineyard. In that period, day laborers gathered in the marketplace early in the morning, hoping one of the landowners would send his foreman to hire them for a day's work. In Jesus' parable, the landowner himself went to the marketplace and hired the workers (20:1). The initiative was with him. He sought the laborers out, rather than the laborers coming to him first.

So it is with the kingdom of God. The initiative is always with God. The writers of the New Testament employed fourteen different verb forms in reference to the kingdom of God, but not once did the writers suggest that people build or establish the kingdom. God declares his sovereign rule over all the earth, and then he invites us to be a part of it. The fact God has allowed us to be a part of his kingdom is due to his generosity.

Notice also that the landowner invited the workers to work in the vineyard at different hours (20:3–7). The Jewish day lasted from 6:00 a.m. to 6:00 p.m., from sunrise to sunset. This landowner, therefore, hired laborers for the vineyard at six in the morning, at nine, at noon, at three in the afternoon, and even at the eleventh hour (5:00 p.m.), when the shadows of sunset were beginning to spread across the land.

Some understand these different hours to symbolize the different stages of human life when people become Christians. At the sunrise of life, still haloed by innocence, a little child can hear the call of God and begin quietly laboring in the vineyard of the kingdom of God. No fanfare. No dramatics. Just a quiet acceptance of God's love in Jesus Christ at a young age.

At noonday, when many of life's experiences have already passed under the bridge, a man or woman can respond to God's Spirit and accept the call to a new life and a new labor. This was true for the Apostle Paul. Even at the evening time, when the shadows of life have grown long, an individual can still become a part of God's kingdom. This was true for the thief on the cross. It is never too late for a person to become a part of the kingdom of God. God calls people to come into his kingdom at different periods of their lives.

Some scholars believe the different hours in the parable represent the different stages of Christian history in which people become members of the kingdom of God. The twelve disciples were with Jesus from the beginning of his ministry. Others turned their attention to him later in his ministry. In terms of the early church, the parable acknowledged the same progressive involvement in the kingdom movement. The Jews in Jerusalem first heard the gospel, then Jews in Palestine, then the Gentiles and the Samaritans, and then Jews of the Diaspora. God calls people to come into his kingdom at different periods of their lives and at different points in history.

The Wages (20:8–10)

Jesus came to the heart of the parable when he described the distribution of the wages for the laborers. At the end of the day, the landowner met with his hired hands to distribute the wages for their work. He first paid the ones who worked only an hour, and he gave them a full day's wage (20:9). He did the same to all of the other groups of workers, even the laborers who had been working since the first hour (20:10). What does this say about God?

The point is not that everyone received the same reward. The point is God's grace provided for everyone. The early workers received their reward. They were amply compensated. Nothing was taken away from them just because the others received the same amount. The landowner also compensated the latecomers. When we labor for God, we can depend on his generosity. No one who labors for God will be without reward.

Jewish literature also features a parable of a landowner and his workers. According to this rabbinical story, a landowner had laborers in the field. One man did so well in the early hours the landowner took him out of the field to travel with him from field to field. At the end of the day, the man who had only worked a short time received the same wages as the others. To the protests of the workers, the landowner replied, "This laborer has done more in two hours than you have done during the whole day."[1]

The response of the landowner in the rabbinical parable reflects a radically different concept of God than Jesus introduced. In the rabbinical version, the laborer of two hours worked harder and thus fully earned his wages. This laborer was an altogether worthy worker. The purpose of the rabbinical parable was to extol the excellence of the laborer in his work. In Jesus' parable, the focus was on the landowner's loving response to his workers. The purpose of Jesus' parable was not to extol the laborer but to glory in the generosity of God.

F.B. Meyer

F. B. Meyer (1847–1929) enjoyed a lifelong preaching ministry that included a number of Baptist churches in England. On twelve trips to North America, an itinerant ministry took him to Baptist churches and Christian conferences throughout the United States. Eventually, however, two other London preachers overshadowed his ministry: Charles Spurgeon (1834–1892) and G. Campbell Morgan (1863–1945). Meyer never begrudged their greater blessings but instead recognized the lavish generosity of God's blessings. He said on one occasion:

"I find in my own ministry that supposing I pray for my own little flock, 'God bless me, God fill my pews, God send me a revival,' I miss the blessing, but as I pray for my big brother, Mr. Spurgeon, on the right-hand side of my church, 'God bless him;' or my other big brother Campbell Morgan, on the other side of my church, 'God bless him,' I am sure to get a blessing without praying for it, for the overflow of their cups fills my little bucket."[2]

The Explanation (20:11–16)

In response to the lavish generosity of God, some of the workers protested (20:11–12). Those who worked all day felt snubbed because they received the same wages as those who only worked the last hour of the day. The land-owner reminded the all-day laborers he paid them exactly what he promised to pay them, so they had no right to complain. If he chose to pay the other workers similar wages, they had no right to question the generosity of the landowner (20:13–15).

Jesus used this parable and the landowner's response to warn his followers against two attitudes reflected by the laborers who had been in the field all day. First, he warned against the attitude of calculation. When we approach God on a *quid pro quo* legalistic basis, we will never experience the generosity of God. We will get our reward, but we will never know the lavish abundance of having the blessing of God "pressed down, shaken together and running over" (Luke 6:38). The point of the parable is that God is not a tyrant to appease, but a father to serve lovingly. We do not need to bargain with him. We need to serve him and trust him to take care of us.

Jesus also used this parable and the landowner's response to warn his followers against the attitude of comparison. When someone receives a blessing, we can balk at those blessings because we feel more worthy of the blessings. "What about us?" we ask God. "Why don't we get those blessings?" The point of the parable is we will never be able to see the goodness of God through jealous eyes. Instead, we must approach God with an attitude of gratitude. Then, as a citizen in the kingdom of heaven, we will not begrudge

Case Study

As a charter member of your church, you have a sense of entitlement about the decision-making process of the church. However, a middle-aged couple joins the church and immediately begins to exert their influence over the congregation. How does the lesson of Jesus' parable affect the way you respond to the growing influence of these newcomers to your church?

the reward given to others. Instead, we will realize the blessed privilege of walking with God and sharing in his work is a lavish act of love in itself. As a latecomer in the kingdom of heaven, we will not flaunt God's grace; rather, we will regret every hour we missed walking in the company of the One who is life.

Live It Out

In this parable, Jesus reminded his listeners of two central truths about God. First, Jesus highlighted the generosity of God. Whatever we receive from God is more than we deserve. Justice is what we deserve; lavish generosity is what we experience. Second, Jesus affirmed the sovereignty of God. Like the landowner in the parable, God can choose to express his generosity in any way he wants. Even though the landowner paid the early workers exactly what he promised them, their sense of fairness did not determine the landowner's response to others. He was free to respond in any manner he chose. In the same way, the sovereign God is free to respond to each person as he determines, not according to our sense of justice or fairness.

Questions

1. Did the workers who had labored all day and were paid the same as those who worked for only an hour have any justification for their protest against the landowner?

2. How is your personal story of kingdom involvement similar to the laborers who came to work in the vineyard at different times?

3. If you came in early to kingdom work (came to Christ at an early age), what are some of the unique blessings that came to you in your service for God?

4. If you came in late to kingdom work (came to Christ at a later age), what are some of the blessings you have experienced?

5. When and how have you experienced the lavish generosity of God?

6. What is the antidote for the jealousy that could creep in when you see God bless others in a different way than he has blessed you?

Notes

1. Craig. S. Keener, *The Gospel of Matthew: A Socio-Rhetorical Commentary* (Grand Rapids, Michigan: Wm. B. Eerdmans Publishing Co., 2009), 484.

2. W.Y. Fullerton, *No Ordinary Man: The Remarkable Life of F.B. Meyer* (Belfast: Ambassador Productions LTD, 1993 reprint, originally published in 1929), 132.

The Passion of the King

Unit Four, "The Passion of the King" contains three lessons covering the events of the final hours of King Jesus' life, as well as his resurrection and the commission he has given to his followers. Lesson eleven describes how Jesus did not deny his identity as he submitted to his Father's plan during his arrest and trials. Lesson twelve recounts the details of Jesus' crucifixion and death as he paid for our sin upon a cross. Lesson thirteen details the glorious resurrection of King Jesus as he defeated death and then commissioned his followers to make disciples of all nations.

lesson 11

The Arrest and Trials of the King

MAIN IDEA

Jesus did not deny his identity as he submitted to his Father's plan during his arrest and trials.

QUESTION TO EXPLORE

How can we imitate Jesus' example of obedience to the Father's plan for our lives?

STUDY AIM

To obey the Father's plan for my life in the midst of difficult circumstances

QUICK READ

Matthew presented Jesus as the true King who was arrested, confronted by Jewish and Roman leaders in unjust trials, and crucified by the people he came to save.

DISCOVER
BIBLE STUDY GUIDE
BELIEVE
LIVE

Introduction

Many years ago, I sat on the jury of a criminal case. According to his custom, the judge instructed the jury regarding circumstantial evidence. In some criminal cases, the circumstantial evidence does not carry the same weight as direct evidence like fingerprints or DNA. Those on trial typically become very defensive when circumstantial evidence is presented, because that evidence could be taken out of context or could be manipulated at the hands of a crafty lawyer.

In the trial of Jesus in the Gospel of Matthew, we witness a steady flow of accusations and misleading evidence. However, we note one shocking aspect of this trial. Jesus was never defensive, not even when the circumstantial evidence against him was unfounded and fabricated. Why? Because Jesus, the divine King, was not nervous about the outcome of the trial. He was following the plan of his Heavenly Father, so the verdict wasn't in the hands of the religious leaders who hated him. The plan had already been set in place and the trial was just a part of the cosmic drama unfolding.[1]

Matthew 26:47–50, 57–66; 27:11–26

47 While he was still speaking, Judas, one of the twelve, arrived; with him was a large crowd with swords and clubs, from the chief priests and the elders of the people. **48** Now the betrayer had given them a sign, saying, "The one I will kiss is the man; arrest him." **49** At once he came up to Jesus and said, "Greetings, Rabbi!" and kissed him. **50** Jesus said to him, "Friend, do what you are here to do." Then they came and laid hands on Jesus and arrested him.

•   •   •   •   •   •   •   •   •   •   •   •   •   •   •   •   •   •

57 Those who had arrested Jesus took him to Caiaphas the high priest, in whose house the scribes and the elders had gathered. **58** But Peter was following him at a distance, as far as the courtyard of the high priest; and going inside, he sat with the guards in order to see how this would end. **59** Now the chief priests and the whole council were looking for false testimony against Jesus so that they might put him to death, **60** but they found none, though many false witnesses came forward. At last two came forward [61] and said, "This fellow said, "I am able to destroy the temple of God and to build it in three days.'"

[62] The high priest stood up and said, "Have you no answer? What is it that they testify against you?" [63] But Jesus was silent. Then the high priest said to him, "I put you under oath before the living God, tell us if you are the Messiah, the Son of God." [64] Jesus said to him, "You have said so. But I tell you,

> From now on you will see the Son of Man
> > seated at the right hand of Power
> > and coming on the clouds of heaven."

[65] Then the high priest tore his clothes and said, "He has blasphemed! Why do we still need witnesses? You have now heard his blasphemy. [66] What is your verdict?" They answered, "He deserves death."

•   •   •   •   •   •   •   •   •   •   •   •   •   •   •   •   •   •   •   •

[11] Now Jesus stood before the governor; and the governor asked him, "Are you the King of the Jews?" Jesus said, "You say so." [12] But when he was accused by the chief priests and elders, he did not answer. [13] Then Pilate said to him, "Do you not hear how many accusations they make against you?" [14] But he gave him no answer, not even to a single charge, so that the governor was greatly amazed.

[15] Now at the festival the governor was accustomed to release a prisoner for the crowd, anyone whom they wanted. [16] At that time they had a notorious prisoner, called Jesus Barabbas. [17] So after they had gathered, Pilate said to them, "Whom do you want me to release for you, Jesus Barabbas or Jesus who is called the Messiah?" [18] For he realized that it was out of jealousy that they had handed him over. [19] While he was sitting on the judgment seat, his wife sent word to him, "Have nothing to do with that innocent man, for today I have suffered a great deal because of a dream about him." [20] Now the chief priests and the elders persuaded the crowds to ask for Barabbas and to have Jesus killed. [21] The governor again said to them, "Which of the two do you want me to release for you?" And they said, "Barabbas." [22] Pilate said to them, "Then what should I do with Jesus who is called the Messiah?" All of them said, "Let him be crucified!" [23] Then he asked, "Why, what evil has he done?" But they shouted all the more, "Let him be crucified!"

> ²⁴ So when Pilate saw that he could do nothing, but rather that a riot was beginning, he took some water and washed his hands before the crowd, saying, "I am innocent of this man's blood; see to it yourselves." ²⁵ Then the people as a whole answered, "His blood be on us and on our children!" ²⁶ So he released Barabbas for them; and after flogging Jesus, he handed him over to be crucified.

The Capture of a King (26:47–56)

The arrest of Jesus took place in a location called Gethsemane, "olive press" in the Greek. The Gospel of John describes Jesus' arrest as taking place in this garden (John 18:1, 26). Thus, this site where Jesus took his disciples after they had eaten the Passover meal is known as the Garden of Gethsemane. The site was visible from the Temple Mount.

The temple guards arrested Jesus at night so a Jewish pretrial before the Sanhedrin could take place in time for a Roman trial in the morning. Typically, Jerusalem doubled or tripled in size during the time of the Passover due to the number of pilgrims. The Romans sought to maintain peace at all cost. This pretrial was both an occasion for the Jews to confront Jesus' Messianic claims and a way for the Romans to avoid riots.

In first-century Mediterranean culture, men greeted other men with a kiss. It was a sign of respect or friendship. For example, students greeted their rabbis with a kiss. Thus, since Judas greeted Jesus with a kiss (Matt. 26:50), those standing around likely assumed Jesus was the rabbi. Jesus called Judas his friend (26:50). This kiss shows Judas' hypocrisy at its pinnacle. Matthew highlighted this act of hypocrisy to show that Judas had fallen in step with the religious leaders. They rewarded Judas with thirty pieces of silver for joining them.

Friendship carried a different connotation in the ancient Greek world compared to today. The types of friendship in the first century were best understood as either political friendships or family-like friendships. Both types of friendships were based on the concept of reciprocity ("this for that"). Jesus used the idea of family-based friendship in this text, but in a sense of irony rather than conveying intimacy. Two other times in his Gospel,

Matthew used the same word for friendship in a sense of irony (Matt. 20:13; 22:12). Jesus' comment to Judas indicates he was all-knowing and thus was aware of what Judas was about to do. Jesus said, "Friend, for this you are here" (26:50). He allowed the events to unfold without offering any resistance to his arrest. He remained as the sovereign King of the universe and understood the will of the Father, so he continued to follow his Father's plan.

The King's First Trial— Rejected by the Jewish Leaders (26:57–67)

The Jewish trial was more like a pretrial examination than a political trial since only the Roman government had jurisdiction. The religious questioning took place in the courtyard of the palace of the high priest, Caiaphas, and was led by the high priest in the presence of the chief priests and the Sanhedrin. At dawn, the Sanhedrin ratified the prior proceedings. At that time, the Sanhedrin decided to hand over Jesus to Pilate (27:2). Therefore, the trials had two phases—a Jewish religious phase and a Roman legal phase. The examination, the questions, Jesus' response, the charge of blasphemy, and the mockery took place at night. Early in the morning, the chief priests and elders condemned Jesus to death and handed him over to Pilate. This flow of events ensured expediency and averted a commotion that might have led to civil unrest, something the Romans wanted to avoid.

According to Matthew's account, the accusations hurled against Jesus were false. The high priest claimed that Jesus uttered blasphemy (26:65). However, according to the Jewish commentary called the *Mishna*, a person is not guilty of blasphemy unless the divine name has been pronounced. Therefore, Jesus did not commit blasphemy. Moreover, blasphemy required death by stoning (Leviticus 24:16). The high priest was the first one to declare Jesus guilty. Since the *Mishna* maintains that in capital cases lower judges first had to cast their votes, Jesus' Jewish trial did not follow rabbinic protocol.

The high priest apparently scoured the crowd for evidence. Receiving inconsistent testimony—corrupted evidence—he became unnerved. No evidence from contradictory witnesses could be used in a Jewish court. Jesus' claim of tearing down and building back the temple in three days was hardly

Friends in the New Testament

- Jesus was a friend of tax collectors and sinners (Matt. 11:19; Luke 7:34).
- Lazarus was Jesus' friend (John 11:11).
- The crowds threatened to accuse Pilate of not being a friend of Caesar if he freed Jesus (John 19:12).
- Jesus used the concept of friends in his parables (Matt. 20:13; 22:12; Luke 11:5–8; 15:6–9).
- Jesus sent healed people home to their friends (Mark 5:19).
- Jesus predicted that his followers would be betrayed by friends (Luke 21:16).
- Herod and Pilate became friends (Luke 23:12).
- Jesus defined love in terms of laying down one's life for friends (John 15:13).
- Jesus defined friendship (John 15:14, 15).
- Jesus called Judas a friend (Matt. 26:50).
- Believers were called friends (Acts 4:31; 27:3; 3 John 1:15).
- Cornelius gathered his friends (Acts 10:24).
- James wrote that Abraham was called a friend of God (James 2:23).
- James warned against being a friend of the world (James 4:4).

enough to require the death penalty (26:61). Frustrated, the high priest changed tactics, placed Jesus under an oath, and asked him if he was the Messiah. Jesus responded to this question, the only question with sufficient dignity to merit the response of a King.

Jesus replied, "You have said so. But I tell you, From now on you will see the Son of Man seated at the right hand of Power and coming on the clouds of heaven" (26:64). Jesus' prophetic reply placed him in God's Messianic plan as foretold in the Book of Daniel (Daniel 7:13–14). Furthermore, since Jesus said, "I say," which is more appropriately translated "I am saying," he assumed the role of their present judge. This response likely offended the high priest, who presupposed that Jesus was not the Messiah and never seemed to consider the real possibility that he stood before his own Messiah.

The Jewish leaders had Jesus beaten, after which they took him to Pilate. Jesus remained silent and offered no resistance. His silence fulfilled the prophecy of Isaiah 53:7 as he submitted to his Father's plan. Labeled a blasphemer, the people sided with the culturally understood outcome. In the ancient Mediterranean culture, labels were permanent once spoken.

The King's Second Trial— Condemned By the Roman Establishment (27:11–26)

Judea was a Roman province. The governor of Judea had the full power of a prefect. Roman prefects had the power to execute people if necessary to protect or promote Roman interests. Whereas the Romans allowed Jews to execute people for certain religious offenses, such as adultery, the Jewish authorities were required to hand over other cases to the Romans. Therefore, charges from the Jewish courts were converted into accusations the Roman leaders would hate; thereby motivating them to take swift and severe action. This explains why the Jewish leaders claimed Jesus was inciting riots among the people, forbidding the paying of taxes, and claiming to be king.

When Pilate was handed Jesus, he contemplated the information given to him, but he found no fault in Jesus that warranted a death sentence. Pilate immediately sought an escape route and sent Jesus to Herod, who was ruler over Galilee. Herod Antipas only ridiculed Jesus and demanded to witness miracles. He returned Jesus to Pilate. Frustrated and conflicted, Pilate tried desperately to appease the Jewish crowds by having Jesus scourged (a terrible whipping with barbed instruments).

The punishment of flogging was a part of the Roman legal code. Jews allowed only thirty-nine lashes while the Romans determined the number of lashes based on the soldier's stamina. Jesus received thirty-nine lashes, which left him with open wounds that exposed tissue and bones across the back and into the rib and stomach area. Afterward, the Jewish leaders remained angered. Ironically, even Pilate, the corrupt politician, had enough discernment to see the religious leaders' plot. He recognized the

The Garden of Gethsemane

"Gethsemane" means "place of an oil press." The Garden of Gethsemane was an olive grove located on the Mount of Olives. According to Romans 11:16, Jesus is the olive root, supporting every olive branch and every olive in the tree. Olives typically were pressed to obtain oil in groves. Likewise, Jesus underwent great pressure in Gethsemane. It is ironic that Jesus underwent great suffering and agony in the "place of the press."

entire conflict as a struggle for power and control on the part of the religious leaders. In all, Matthew revealed a trial overwhelmed with injustice and absurdity.

Calls for the Crucifixion of King Jesus (27:15–26)

Trying further to appease the Jewish leaders and avoid rioting, Pilate offered to release one Jew according to a custom practiced during the Passover season. Persuaded by the chief priests and the elders, the crowds chose Barabbas, a known criminal (27:20–23), as the one to be released.

Matthew is the only Gospel writer who added to Pilate's reason to seek Jesus' release. His Gentile wife recalled a frightful dream about Jesus and urged Pilate to have nothing to do with him (27:19). Perhaps she deemed Jesus innocent. Perhaps she was afraid their actions might result in politically disadvantageous consequences. Either way, Matthew revealed another Gentile who was convinced of Jesus' innocence.

According to Matthew, all the people shouted to crucify Jesus (27:22), which may well refer to "all the people" mentioned in Matthew 27:25 as well. Their request to crucify Jesus sought to demonstrate that he was under God's curse (Deuteronomy 21:23). Heeding his wife's pleas, Pilate washed his hands, a Jewish act rather than a Roman one (Deut. 21:6–9). However, neutrality never erases guilt before God. The impassioned people demanded the crucifixion of Jesus. Mocking and crucifixion ensued.

Live It Out

As followers of Jesus, we identify with the name, life, and mission of the Lord Jesus. Reflecting upon the account of Jesus' arrest, trial, suffering, and crucifixion, believers are challenged by his calm demeanor during his arrest, his boldness during his unjust trial, and his obedience to the Father during suffering. What would it have been like to witness the shocking betrayal with a kiss? How would we have responded when observing the unfair elements of the Jewish trial and the peer pressure during the Roman trial? Would we bend to cultural demands or give in to peer pressure? As you ponder Jesus' obedience to his Father, consider ways in which you may need to submit to the Father's plan in your life.

Questions

1. What do you think was going through Judas' mind when he betrayed Jesus?

2. Why did Jesus permit his arrest? What do Jesus' actions say about his character?

3. Do you tend to defend yourself when you are accused unfairly? Explain.

4. Do you tend to accept the labels pronounced on people? Explain.

5. Do you think Pilate's wife truly deemed Jesus innocent of his charges, or do you think she had ulterior motives? Explain.

6. Do you think you would have joined the crowd in their request to have Jesus crucified? Explain.

Notes

1. Unless otherwise indicated, all Scripture quotations in lessons 11–13 and the Christmas lesson are from the New Revised Standard Version (1989 edition).

lesson 12

The Crucifixion and Death of the King

MAIN IDEA

Jesus paid for our sin with his death upon a cross.

QUESTION TO EXPLORE

What do the details of Jesus' crucifixion and death reveal about the character of our King?

STUDY AIM

To identify how the details of Jesus' crucifixion and death reveal the character of my King

QUICK READ:

Matthew presented Jesus as the King who drank the cup of suffering and displayed the character of God when mocked and killed for the sins of those who maligned him.

127

Introduction

The oldest written account of Christian martyrdom outside of the New Testament is one of the most touching of all time. In A.D. 156, Polycarp, a bishop of Smyrna who knew the Apostle John, was on trial before a Roman proconsul. When asked to renounce Christ he said, "Eighty and six years have I served Him, and He never did me any injury. How then can I blaspheme my King and Savior?"[1] Those viewing him before his martyrdom testified, "As he spoke these and many other words, he was inspired with courage and joy, and his face was filled with grace, so that not only did he not collapse in fright at the things which were said to him, but on the contrary the proconsul was astonished . . ."[2] Polycarp burned to death before the Romans, demonstrating great grace to the very end. In the text for this study, Jesus faced even greater pressures and extended torture, yet his character remained strong and graceful to the very end.

Matthew 27:32–54

[32] As they went out, they came upon a man from Cyrene named Simon; they compelled this man to carry his cross. [33] And when they came to a place called Golgotha (which means Place of a Skull), [34] they offered him wine to drink, mixed with gall; but when he tasted it, he would not drink it. [35] And when they had crucified him, they divided his clothes among themselves by casting lots; [36] then they sat down there and kept watch over him. [37] Over his head they put the charge against him, which read, "This is Jesus, the King of the Jews."

[38] Then two bandits were crucified with him, one on his right and one on his left. [39] Those who passed by derided him, shaking their heads [40] and saying, "You who would destroy the temple and build it in three days, save yourself! If you are the Son of God, come down from the cross." [41] In the same way the chief priests also, along with the scribes and elders, were mocking him, saying, [42] "He saved others; he cannot save himself. He is the King of Israel; let him come down from the cross now, and we will believe in him. [43] He trusts in God; let God deliver him now, if he wants to; for he said, 'I am God's Son.'" [44] The bandits who were crucified with him also taunted him in the same way.

[45] From noon on, darkness came over the whole land until three in the afternoon. [46] And about three o'clock Jesus cried with a loud voice, "Eli, Eli, lema sabachthani?" that is, "My God, my God, why have you forsaken me?" [47] When some of the bystanders heard it, they said, "This man is calling for Elijah." [48] At once one of them ran and got a sponge, filled it with sour wine, put it on a stick, and gave it to him to drink. [49] But the others said, "Wait, let us see whether Elijah will come to save him." [50] Then Jesus cried again with a loud voice and breathed his last. [51] At that moment the curtain of the temple was torn in two, from top to bottom. The earth shook, and the rocks were split. [52] The tombs also were opened, and many bodies of the saints who had fallen asleep were raised. [53] After his resurrection they came out of the tombs and entered the holy city and appeared to many. [54] Now when the centurion and those with him, who were keeping watch over Jesus, saw the earthquake and what took place, they were terrified and said, "Truly this man was God's Son!"

King Jesus at Golgotha (27:32–37)

As a part of the crucifixion process, Jesus was led out of the city of Jerusalem. The Jews maintained extensive purity laws. For example, Jerusalem was considered a holy city. As part of the purity regimen, bloodshed took place outside of the city walls. Thus, crucifixion took place along a major road outside the city. The writer of the Book of Hebrews connected the concept of sacred space and the crucifixion of Christ outside the city by writing, "For the bodies of those animals whose blood is brought into the sanctuary by the high priest as a sacrifice for sin are burned outside the camp. Therefore, Jesus also suffered outside the city gate" (Hebrews 13:11–12). Jesus was that sacrifice.

Matthew reported the crucifixion procession (including Jesus, the criminals, Roman soldiers, and the crowds) encountered a man by the name of Simon (Matt. 27:32). He was from Cyrene, a person from the capital city of the North African district of Cyrenaica in the area of Libya. Acts 6:9 describes the presence of a Cyrenian synagogue in Jerusalem. Thus, travelers from Cyrene were a common sight in Jerusalem, perhaps especially around Passover. Matthew recorded, "they [the soldiers] compelled this man to carry his [Jesus'] cross (27:32)." The same Greek word that is translated "to carry" was used in Matthew 16:24 as well, but in that usage, the phrase is most often translated as "take up," as in "If any want to become my followers, let them deny themselves and take up their cross and follow me" (16:24).

Jesus was in a weakened state when he arrived with the soldiers at Golgotha, the place of the crucifixion. Not only had Simon of Cyrene been enlisted to carry the crossbar to the place, the soldiers also offered Jesus wine to drink with gall to provide a sedative while they nailed his hands and feet to the cross. The women of Jerusalem customarily prepared such drinks for those who were crucified. Jesus refused to take the sedative. He fulfilled his mission on the cross with his faculties fully intact.

The soldiers who assisted in the execution were allowed by Roman law to confiscate any minor possessions of those whom they crucified. The guards gambled for Jesus' clothing, thereby fulfilling a Messianic psalm (Psalm 22:19). Whereas casting lots was customary, writing up a charge for the condemned was not. However, Pilate (John 19:19) made a special effort to record the charge in the crucifixion of Jesus. Pilate refused the request of the leading priests to change the sign that was hung over Jesus' head. The sign read: "This is Jesus, the King of the Jews" (Matt. 27:37). What was meant as a mark of insult still rings true today.

Why Did Jesus Die?

Why did Jesus die? Jesus' death by crucifixion affected not only those who were present or who lived at the time of his death, but it also carried consequences for the entirety of humanity. Paul stated, "Christ died for our sins" (1 Corinthians 15:3). The New Testament writers described in a variety of ways the significance of Christ's death: to show an example of God's love (Romans 5:8; 1 John 4:10); to be a sin offering (1 Cor. 5:7); to claim a victory over the battle against sin and death (Colossians 2:8–15; John 12:31); to act as a ransom for the sin of humanity (Mark 10:45; 1 Peter 2:24); to take the place of others (1 Pet. 2:24); and to take the shame of humanity upon himself (Philippians 2:8–9).

The Romans did not invent crucifixion, nor was it originally intended as a method of execution. Initially, it was used as a punishment tool for runaway slaves and insurrectionists. The Romans, however, perfected its use and adopted it as a means of execution. Moreover, they used it as a way of inflicting utmost shame. This included mocking the person, crucifying the person fully naked, dividing up the person's belongings, and leaving the bodies to be eaten by wild animals. Families were so ashamed by this manner of execution that the bodies rarely were claimed and instead were thrown into mass graves. Jesus was naked as he hung on the cross. This humiliation was intensified by the sight of the brutality done to Jesus' body when he was flogged.

Crucifixion took place against a tree or a vertical structure that allowed for the attachment of a crossbeam. The offender was tied to the crossbeam and nails were used to affix the victim's wrists fully to the cross. The feet were nailed to the cross-shaped structure as well. The victims would struggle for air. Eventually, the victims could no longer push their bodies upward to breathe, and the loss of oxygen combined with the buildup of carbon dioxide and loss of blood became too much. Crucifixion ultimately resulted in death from suffocation.

King Jesus Mocked (27:38–44)

Three groups of people mocked and insulted Jesus—the people who passed by, the priests, and the people crucified beside him. The insults had a common theme, "Come down from the cross if you are the Son of God" (27:40). These taunts were similar to those Satan hurled during Jesus' temptation: "If you are the Son of God" (Matt. 4:3). Jesus rejected Satan's offer of political power. Jesus also rejected political power before and during his crucifixion. Jesus' kingdom and the salvation of mankind required his sacrificial death.

The people likely passed by on a road beside which Jesus was crucified. The priests quoted from Psalm 22:8, "Commit your cause to the Lord; let him deliver—let him rescue the one in whom he delights!" In doing so, they appeared to insult God himself. The priests uttered these taunts among themselves in an effort to deny the claims of Christ. Even the thieves crucified with Jesus insulted him.

King Jesus Died (27:45–50)

At noon, darkness fell on the land. This darkness was a sign of judgment that signified the weight of the sin of the world that Jesus bore upon the cross. The prophet Amos had prophesied concerning this day: "On that day, says the Lord God, I will make the sun go down at noon, and darken the earth in broad daylight" (Amos 8:9).

In the hours during which Jesus hung on the cross, he made many statements that revealed the essence of his character. Though Jesus hung in great pain, he spoke with compassion to people and intimately to his Father. He arranged for the daily care of his mother (John 19:26–27). Thirst brought on the request of vinegar (John 19:28). Jesus forgave his executors (Luke 23:34). At about three o'clock he cried, *Eloi, Eloi, lama sabachthani*, which is interpreted as, "My God, my God, why have you forsaken me?" (27:46). Bystanders misinterpreted Jesus' words as a call for Elijah (who went to heaven without dying; see 2 Kings 2:1–12). Jesus not only endured the darkest crucible of physical agony, but he also experienced spiritual separation from his Father—the ultimate torture—as expressed in his utterance.

One of the soldiers, who like some of the bystanders thought Jesus was calling for Elijah, offered Jesus sour wine (Matt. 27:48). The wine vinegar might have revived him somewhat. However, Jesus was determined to drink the cup of suffering that had been placed before him.

The Power of the King's Death (27:51–54)

Matthew described Jesus' last words while he was giving a loud cry and breathing his last (27:50). This loud cry likely was "It is finished!" as recorded in John 19:30. John also recorded that Jesus "gave up his Spirit" (John 19:30). The idea of "giving up" or "yielding up" in the original language focuses on the person performing an intentional act. The focus was not on how Jesus gave up his Spirit but on the fact he was in control of giving up his life. Because of the magnitude of this moment, heaven and earth reverberated with strange phenomena: earthquakes rocked the city, tombs were opened, and corpses walked around the streets of Jerusalem (27:51–53).

Golgotha

The name "Golgotha" is the Jewish name for the place of crucifixion. The Latin Vulgate, an early Latin translation of the Bible, translated the phrase *Calvariae locum*, "Place of the Skull." Some have suggested that this location (a hill) had the shape of a skull. The English term "calvary" derives from this Latin phrase. The different Gospel accounts contain these various names.

Something significant also took place at the temple. The Holy Place was located in the center of the temple complex. The Holy Place contained the Holy of Holies, the space that represented the presence of God. A curtain divided the two spaces. At the moment Jesus died, the curtain tore in two, an indication that all people could now have direct access to God because of Jesus' sacrificial death on the cross. Significantly, it was torn from top to bottom, symbolizing God had made it possible to come to him; no human effort could accomplish such a feat.

The centurion and those with him were terrified when they experienced phenomena such as the earthquake. The centurion, likely terrified of impending judgment, exclaimed that Jesus' claims held true (27:54). The Son of God had died. His divine character was revealed while undergoing the most excruciating pain. Extraordinarily hurt and shamed on the cross, he had continued his intimacy with the Father. This is a timeless lesson to encourage Christians to remain faithful.

Live It Out

Believers are members of God's kingdom, a kingdom inaugurated by suffering. How often do we reflect upon the nature of this kingdom? Do we expect a reign of success? Do we look for earthly achievement and affirmation? Or do we remember and anticipate the mocking and taunting the Lord Jesus received? Jesus received harsh treatment from people of every social grouping and yet remained true to his mission. How do we respond to hardship in our lives? Do we reflect the character of Jesus?

Questions

1. In your view, what part of the crucifixion of Jesus caused the worst suffering: the physical pain, the social shame, the spiritual anguish, or something else? Why?

2. Which one of Jesus' actions or statements on the cross causes you the most amazement? Why?

3. Give an example of an Old Testament prophecy that was fulfilled in Jesus' death on the cross.

4. How does the crucifixion and death of Jesus relate to your life?

Notes

1. Polycarp 9.3 as found at
   http://www.earlychristianwritings.com/text/martyrdompolycarp-roberts.html.
   Accessed 7/23/15.
2. Ibid., Polycarp 12.1.

lesson 13

The Resurrection and Commission of the King

MAIN IDEA

Jesus defeated death and commissioned his followers to make disciples of all nations.

QUESTIONS TO EXPLORE

Have I placed my faith in King Jesus? How am I making disciples of all nations?

STUDY AIM

To place my faith in King Jesus and to be actively involved in making disciples of all nations

QUICK READ:

Matthew presented Jesus as the living King who desires a relationship with all people and seeks obedient followers to share the Good News of his kingdom with individuals of all nations.

DISCOVER
BELIEVE
LIVE
BIBLE STUDY GUIDE

Introduction

In the lovely mountains of Colorado, my father's mission group took its customary day to enjoy the scenery. One mountain scene was so lovely the driver pulled into a scenic overlook. The view was eye-popping. Amidst camera clicks and "ooh's and ahh's," my dad noticed a young man in his twenties standing at the edge of the precipice. After a while, Dad mustered his bravery, walked over to the young man, and inquired about his day.

He was met with little response. Dad said, "I thought I might want talk to you since you're about twenty-one-years-old, the same as my son." The young man said, "Yes, that was an amazing guess." After exchanging other pleasantries, Dad stumbled through an awkward description of the difference living for Christ had made in his life during his recent battles with cancer. The young man said, "Mister, you won't believe this, but I'm a tour guide on this mountain and have felt so lost lately. I came up here today to jump off this overlook and end my life." Right then and there, the young man accepted the living Savior. The kingdom of heaven had invaded that young man's soul.

On numerous occasions, Jesus spoke of the kingdom of heaven coming to earth. He anticipated this kingdom as the very goal of existence and destiny of human history. God's love would reign in the hearts of his followers. The resurrection of Christ made this kingdom a present reality, the pivotal moment of all history. Christ is alive today and rules his kingdom!

Matthew 28:1–10, 16–20

[1] After the sabbath, as the first day of the week was dawning, Mary Magdalene and the other Mary went to see the tomb. [2] And suddenly there was a great earthquake; for an angel of the Lord, descending from heaven, came and rolled back the stone and sat on it. [3] His appearance was like lightning, and his clothing white as snow. [4] For fear of him the guards shook and became like dead men. [5] But the angel said to the women, "Do not be afraid; I know that you are looking for Jesus who was crucified. [6] He is not here; for he has been raised, as he said. Come, see the place where he lay. [7] Then go quickly and tell his disciples, "He

has been raised from the dead, and indeed he is going ahead of you to Galilee; there you will see him.' This is my message for you." [8] So they left the tomb quickly with fear and great joy, and ran to tell his disciples. [9] Suddenly Jesus met them and said, "Greetings!" And they came to him, took hold of his feet, and worshiped him. [10] Then Jesus said to them, "Do not be afraid; go and tell my brothers to go to Galilee; there they will see me."

•   •   •   •   •   •   •   •   •   •   •   •   •   •   •   •   •   •   •

[16] Now the eleven disciples went to Galilee, to the mountain to which Jesus had directed them. [17] When they saw him, they worshiped him; but some doubted. [18] And Jesus came and said to them, "All authority in heaven and on earth has been given to me. [19] Go therefore and make disciples of all nations, baptizing them in the name of the Father and of the Son and of the Holy Spirit, [20] and teaching them to obey everything that I have commanded you. And remember, I am with you always, to the end of the age."

King Jesus is Alive! (28:1–10)

Very early on that fateful Sunday morning, women traveled to the tomb to see if someone might open the tomb so they could anoint Jesus' body with spices. In the minds of the disciples and the women, Jesus was sealed away in a tomb. Tombs of first-century Palestine were rounded openings hewn out of solid rock. A shaft led slightly underground to a small room with smaller shafts or ledges where the bodies were stored.

The Saturday Sabbath day ended at daybreak. Only then were the women free to approach the tomb. Matthew mentioned an earthquake as an angel descended, rolled back the stone, and sat on it (28:2). Earthquakes were viewed as signs of divine activity. The women arrived at the tomb in time to view the divine activity. The angel's task was not to raise Jesus from the dead or to let him out of the tomb, but to reveal the contents of the tomb.

The guards shook for fear like dead men (28:4). Doubtless, the women were fearful, which is probably why the angel comforted them (28:5–6).

Their hearts were likely overwhelmed with conflicting emotions. Perhaps there was anxiety mingled with newfound joy, or doubts overshadowing the possibility of good news. Could Jesus be alive? Could it be that images of Jesus' pale body, still hanging on the cross, remained imprinted in their minds? They had been at the cross and had seen him die, but they could not deny the angel's appearance and message.

The angel told the women Jesus "had been raised." The way in which this is worded in the original language conveyed an outside agent had accomplished the resurrection. The Father raised Jesus from the dead. The angel instructed the women to go to Galilee to tell Jesus' disciples. The witness of women was considered unreliable in that culture. God's plan in the witness of the women was refreshingly countercultural. Women were sent to preach the good news of the resurrected Christ to the men. Not only that, but Jesus appeared first before the women, enforcing the countercultural scene and validating the place of women in God's economy.

The women left the tomb in fear and great joy. Following the angel's directions, they ran to relay the news to the disciples. On the way, Jesus suddenly greeted them. The response of the women was dramatic: they bowed and touched his feet and worshiped him. Falling at someone's feet indicated deep reverence; while worshiping signified the presence of deity. Jesus reiterated the message of the angel and told the women to share the news of his resurrection (28:8–10). Jesus instructed that henceforth women and men would share the Good News. Note the women shared the news and sent "Jesus' brothers" to Galilee (28:10) as instructed.

King Jesus Commissions his Followers (28:11–20)

Before continuing to tell the resurrection story, Matthew noted during this history-altering moment, the chief priests and Jewish elders were striking a deal in the backrooms of Jerusalem. The Jewish leaders consulted with the soldiers to concoct a story of how the disciples had taken the body of Jesus during the night. The elders sweetened the deal with a "large sum of money" (28:12). This conspiracy between the Jewish leaders and the soldiers demonstrated the great lengths to which the Jewish leaders would go to snuff out any further talk of Jesus as the Messiah.

After mentioning the deal between the elders and soldiers, Matthew flashed forward to a mountain in Galilee where the eleven disciples and others met the Lord. They had traveled to Galilee in obedience. Note these disciples had first met Jesus in Galilee, but when they met him there again, he was the resurrected King. Matthew was careful to note that when the disciples saw Jesus, they worshiped, but "some were doubtful" (28:17).

Perhaps it was no wonder "some doubted." Bodily resurrection was not a part of the Judaism belief system of that day. Only a future, universal resurrection was believed to occur at the end of history. Only later would they see Jesus' resurrection as "first fruits" of the final resurrection of all saints. Lazarus would die again, but Jesus' bodily resurrection brought a new hope to all humanity.

Mark, Luke, and John recorded other encounters with Jesus. Luke told of two men who met Jesus on their way to Emmaus (Luke 24:13–35). John chronicled Jesus' appearance to Thomas (John 20:24–29) and Jesus' restoring Peter (John 21:1–23). In the Book of Acts, Luke wrote of how Jesus presented himself to many other people over forty days, convincing them of his resurrection (Acts 1:2–3). At the end of those forty days, Jesus gathered the disciples at an appointed mountain. There, he commissioned the early believers to make disciples of all nations (Matt. 28:19–20).

Note Matthew's Gospel opens with Gentile Magi coming from a far-away nation to find the Savior. This same Gospel closes with Jesus' command to

An Urgent Commission

In Matthew 28:19–20, the verbs "going," "baptizing," and "teaching" flow from the main verb "making disciples." The phrase translated as "go therefore" at the beginning of verse 19 has been translated as a simple participle in some Bible translations, interpreting the phrase as, "as you are going, make disciples of all the nations." While this is an accurate translation, the phrase "go therefore" is also an imperative participle—a participle meant as a command. Thus, the phrase could be translated, "Get going! Make disciples!" Herod used the same verb form when he said, "Go and search carefully for the young child" (Matt. 2:8). Herod implied immediate action. The same immediacy is emphasized in Matthew 28:19–20.

take the gospel to far-away places. These disciples were to travel the world to reach people in all areas and of all ethnicities with Jesus' teachings. That call to disciple-making applies to all Christians, not just clergy. Baptizing in the name of the Father, the Son, and the Holy Spirit; along with teaching, are part of disciple-making. Matthew highlighted Jesus' place beside the Father and the Holy Spirit as deity. Baptism became the symbol of conversion.

Jesus' promise to be with his disciples "always, to the end of the age" (28:20) might seem like a contradiction since Jesus was about to leave. However, since he has "all authority" (28:18) in creation, he can exert that authority with his continual presence—a comforting and empowering presence—as we make disciples. While this statement was comforting, it was also shocking. The ancient Near Eastern and Mesopotamian deities and the Greco-Roman gods were localized deities. They were restricted to ruling over a city, the underworld, a body of water, the temple, Jerusalem, a task (harvest, health, procreation), and so forth. Jesus clearly identified himself as the omnipresent (everywhere present) creator God, the one who would not

Responses to the Resurrection

- The women departed from the empty tomb with fear and great joy.
- The guards at the tomb were terrified and became like dead men when they saw the angel at the tomb.
- The chief priests and elders bribed the soldiers to lie and said the disciples had stolen Jesus' body.
- The disciples went to Galilee and worshiped Jesus, but some doubted.
- Peter went fishing until Jesus met him and restored him.
- Thomas demanded to touch Jesus' hands and side.
- The men from Emmaus didn't recognize Jesus until he broke bread with them.

What is your response to the resurrection?

remain confined to any one place. He promised to go with the believers into all the nations because he is God Almighty.

History testifies to how the initial disciples conveyed this authority and presence. After that fateful Sunday, these once-fearful disciples witnessed of the risen Christ with reckless abandon for the rest of their lives. They were committed to Jesus as King over all of life. Their lives are a testimony that when you believe in Jesus as the Lord, your eternal and life purposes are altered toward abandoned service unto him.

Live It Out

The resurrection of Jesus forever changed the course of human history. No longer does death have the final word. It is no longer the ultimate victor. The risen King is alive, victorious over all, and continues to reign today. Some respond to the Good News with fear and trembling; others respond with great joy. For those who have embraced Jesus' loving invitation and have joined his kingdom, a commission calls them to share the story of the risen Christ with a world in need.

How can we live in such a way as to make disciples of all the nations and baptize them into the family of God? Are we willing to put aside our prejudices and comfort? Do we indeed love God and love our neighbor? Do we realize the Holy Spirit will be present with us until the end of the age? This passage calls us to reflect on these questions, and then to take action to complete Christ's commission.

Questions

1. In what ways do we experience the kingdom of God as a present reality?

2. Why was Matthew careful to make the point "some were doubtful" about Jesus' resurrection?

3. Since the witness of women was deemed unreliable in that culture, why do you think Jesus appeared to them first?

4. In what ways are the resurrections of Jesus and Lazarus similar? In what ways are they different?

5. In what ways are you obeying Jesus' command to make disciples of all nations?

6. What about making disciples is scary or uncomfortable for you?

Christmas Lesson

When Faith Becomes Sight

MAIN IDEA

Two faithful servants of God meet their long-awaited Messiah and respond with praise and thanksgiving.

QUESTION TO EXPLORE

How should we respond to the arrival of the Messiah?

STUDY AIM

To respond to Jesus' birth with praise and thanksgiving for the salvation he brings

QUICK READ

Luke presented the promised arrival of the Savior as a joyous event that changes everything in life and is met with exuberant praise and thanksgiving.

DISCOVER
BELIEVE
LIVE
BIBLE STUDY GUIDE

Introduction

If you were honest, what thoughts go through your mind each year as Christmas draws near? I imagine many of us think, "Oh my, I have so much work to do!" Or, "I wonder whose homes will we visit and when?" Or even, "I wish we could just stay home this year." Perhaps these thoughts and questions make Christmas feel overwhelming or cause it to lose its luster.

However, what if the holiday were approached differently? What if sheer excitement and expectation marked the advent of Christmas? In this lesson, two elderly people had anticipated a special Christmas for decades upon decades. At last, their heart's desire became reality. We will discover sometimes the greatest journey in life is moving toward seeing Christ and then responding to his presence with praise and thanksgiving.

Luke 2:21–38

21 After eight days had passed, it was time to circumcise the child; and he was called Jesus, the name given by the angel before he was conceived in the womb.

22 When the time came for their purification according to the law of Moses, they brought him up to Jerusalem to present him to the Lord 23 (as it is written in the law of the Lord, "Every firstborn male shall be designated as holy to the Lord"), 24 and they offered a sacrifice according to what is stated in the law of the Lord, "a pair of turtledoves or two young pigeons."

25 Now there was a man in Jerusalem whose name was Simeon; this man was righteous and devout, looking forward to the consolation of Israel, and the Holy Spirit rested on him. 26 It had been revealed to him by the Holy Spirit that he would not see death before he had seen the Lord's Messiah. 27 Guided by the Spirit, Simeon came into the temple; and when the parents brought in the child Jesus, to do for him what was customary under the law, 28 Simeon took him in his arms and praised God, saying,

29 "Master, now you are dismissing your servant in peace,
     according to your word;
30 for my eyes have seen your salvation,

31 which you have prepared in the presence of all peoples,
32 a light for revelation to the Gentiles
and for glory to your people Israel."
33 And the child's father and mother were amazed at what was being said about him. 34 Then Simeon blessed them and said to his mother Mary, "This child is destined for the falling and the rising of many in Israel, and to be a sign that will be opposed 35 so that the inner thoughts of many will be revealed—and a sword will pierce your own soul too."
36 There was also a prophet, Anna the daughter of Phanuel, of the tribe of Asher. She was of a great age, having lived with her husband seven years after her marriage, 37 then as a widow to the age of eighty-four. She never left the temple but worshiped there with fasting and prayer night and day. 38 At that moment she came, and began to praise God and to speak about the child to all who were looking for the redemption of Jerusalem.

The Jewish Rites for the Newborn (2:21–24)

The text begins with the parents of Jesus from Nazareth fulfilling the requirements of the Jewish law concerning their newborn child. Paul would later write to the Galatians that the Savior was born under the law in order to redeem those who were under the law (Galatians 4:4). The same law drew Jesus' family to the temple just after Jesus' birth. On the eighth day, they circumcised him in accordance with the ceremonial law (Leviticus 12:2–3).

Circumcision is first mentioned in the Bible as a sign of the covenant between God and Abraham (Genesis 17:10). Circumcision and naming often went hand-in-hand. Zechariah confirmed publically the name of John the Baptist at the moment John was circumcised on the eight day (Luke 1:59–64), an indication of paternal acceptance of a child associated with the rite of circumcision. It was also a declaration of paternal responsibility to raise this child in the religious community. Only a circumcised male could participate in the Passover or worship in the court of the Jewish males in the temple in Jerusalem.

Jesus' circumcision (which did not take place in Jerusalem) did not complete the ritual requirements for a firstborn child. An additional forty-day period lapsed, during which the mother underwent her purification (Lev. 12:2–4). Upon completion of that purification period, the child could be presented to the Lord in the Jerusalem temple.

The presentation of Jesus took place because he was the first-born, the opener of the womb. Every male who opened the womb was called holy unto the Lord (Exodus 13:2, 12, 15; Numbers 18:15). Whereas Luke made no mention of it, the parents likely paid five shekels to redeem the first-born (Num. 18:15). The angel of the Lord had instructed to name Mary's baby, "Jesus" (Luke 1:30–31). The law required a lamb and a pigeon to be sacrificed. The parents provided these animals to the priests for the customary sin offering.

On the appointed day, Mary and Joseph presented the child Jesus in the temple in Jerusalem. The text mentions they brought him "up" to Jerusalem (Luke 2:22). Jerusalem was located on an elevated plateau with the temple built on a mount. Notice the young couple provided only a pigeon (2:24), the minimum requirement according to Leviticus 12:8. This modest sacrifice tells us the couple was poor. Joseph, Jesus' earthly father, was a carpenter

Herod's Temple

Solomon's Temple was destroyed in 586 B.C. (2 Chronicles 36), partly rebuilt and dedicated by the Jews who returned from exile (515 B.C.), and slightly extended during the Hasmonean period (152–137 B.C.). Herod the Great rebuilt the temple during the Roman reign over Israel. This is the same temple in which Jesus was dedicated.

At the center of the temple stood the Holy Place, which contained the Holy of Holies which was divided from the remainder of the Holy Place by a curtain. In an adjacent court, the priest offered sacrifices. The Court of Israel was located outside this area, which was accessible only to Jewish males. Women were not allowed into the temple area. Since the parents presented the baby together to Simeon, Simeon most likely stood in the court of the women (Luke 2:27–35), which was next to the court of the men. The overall temple area covered about thirty-five acres and was located on a hilltop.

or an artisan in wood, stone, or metal. The couple could not afford the pre-ferred lamb, nor did it have land on which to raise one.

According to the law, the sacrifice would bring divine appeasement as the animal bore the guilt of sin. In this special case, unknown to all, the animal atoned only for the sins of the mother and father. Jesus was sinless and would become the ultimate atoning sacrifice for all humankind. As Mary and Joseph were bringing the baby before the priests for the final ritual of purification, Simeon and Anna, aged fixtures of the temple, were standing in proximity. They had waited for decades for the coming of Israel's Messiah.

Simeon Meets the Messiah (2:25–35)

The Scripture describes Simeon as waiting patiently, eagerly anticipating the Deliverer. Simeon would have been lost to history except for Luke's account, where he wrote, "Now there was a man in Jerusalem called Simeon, who was righteous and devout. He was waiting for the consolation of Israel, and the Holy Spirit was upon him" (2:25). The Old Testament prophets antici-pated this consolation or comfort. Simeon had waited to see the deliverance of Israel during his lifetime, the consolation of his people. The prophet Isaiah had prophesied this event many centuries prior saying, "Shout for joy, O heavens; rejoice, O earth; burst into song, O mountains! For the LORD comforts his people and will have compassion on his afflicted ones" (Isaiah 49:13).

The Messiah would bring this comfort to Simeon. Hence, Simeon's con-fidence was not guesswork. He had received a word from the Holy Spirit confirming he would see the Messiah during his lifetime (Luke 2:26). The Spirit guided Simeon into the temple in order to set up a providential meet-ing between the Messiah and the one who expected him (2:27).

Simeon was one of many Jews in Israel in the first century who longed for a return of the glories of Israel. In that day, various sects of Jews populated Israel, looking for God's intervention on their behalf. Each sect anticipated its own means of achieving Israel's return to glory. Some sided with the Romans (the Herodians), while others sought to merit God's intervention by exacting obedience to their traditions (the Pharisees). Still others sanc-tified themselves by withdrawing to desert caves (the Essenes). Simeon's

single-minded devotion to God (and not a religious group) led him to fre-
quent the Jerusalem temple for God's comfort, the coming of the awaited
Messiah. This anticipation was central to his faith.

Simeon was in the temple because of the presence of God and was labeled
as "devout," meaning he carefully guarded his relationship with God.
Because of this Spirit-led component and a faithful relationship with the
Father, the Lord blessed Simeon. As Mary and Joseph entered the temple
with baby Jesus, Simeon took the child into his arms and blessed him. Then
he was ready to die, because his life's goal had been accomplished. He had
held the baby Jesus, his Messiah, in his arms. He was at perfect peace. His
devotion begs us to ask ourselves: Are we willing to wait for God's promises
to become reality? Can we wait and hold onto our devotion? Are we at peace
with allowing God to provide our fulfillment in his timing and to work his
purposes in us as he sees fit?

Simeon prophesied salvation would come to all people, and the Jews would
be a "Light to the Gentiles." Unlike most of the sects of the day, Simeon's
message revealed an unprejudiced heart. God gave Simeon a special word for
Mary (2:34–35).

Simeon told Mary a sword would pierce her soul because of her being the
mother of the long-awaited Messiah. This prophecy has been interpreted in

Female Prophets in the Bible:

- The prophet Miriam, Aaron's sister (Exodus 15:20).

- The prophetess and judge, Deborah, wife of Lappidoth
  (Judges 4:4).

- The prophetess Huldah, the wife of Shallum, from Jerusalem
  (2 Kings 22:14).

- Isaiah's wife, the prophetess (Isaiah 8:2).

- The prophet and widow Anna, the daughter of Phanuel, from the
  tribe of Asher, who served in the Jerusalem temple (Luke 2:36).

- The four unmarried daughters of Philip the evangelist, named in
  Acts as having the gift of prophecy (Acts 21:9).

- Female prophets in the early church (1 Corinthians 11:5).

a variety of ways. Some scholars conclude Mary would suffer martyrdom. However, many doubt that interpretation. Instead, other scholars conclude the reference to being pierced referred to the sharp pains of seeing the crucifixion. Yet another interpretation determines the phrase "the sword will pierce" was a reference to unbelief. However, we have almost no evidence of Mary's unbelief, apart from a vague reference in Mark 3:31.

Most likely, the prophecy was meant to brace Mary as she supported her son in the hard-fought struggle to redeem Israel. Jesus would cause the rise and fall of many and divide the faithful from the faithless. All of this, plus his awful crucifixion, would pierce her soul deeply. As Simeon looked into the eyes of an anxious teenage girl, he saw a tumultuous life was in store for this young mother of the Messiah.

The Prophetess Anna (2:36–38)

In verse 36, Luke recorded the story of another devoted Jew who also resided in the temple day after day: Anna, a prophetess. No prophet had been in Israel for hundreds of years. Thus, God raised up this prophetess for this very occasion. As such, she foretold the future at times but also preached to the people the ways of God in their present situation. In the eyes of onlookers, God gave her revelation in the same manner as he did to Deborah (Judges 4) or Hulda (2 Kings 22:14–20) in the Old Testament.

Anna was a unique individual. In her early years, she had experienced deep heartache. She had been married only seven years when her husband passed away. She spent the remainder of her life as a single adult who was devoted to God alone. Anna was of considerable age. If she were married at the typical age of thirteen, she would have been about 104-years-old (Scripture says she had been a widow for 84 years). According to Luke, Anna never left the temple. Women typically did not spend the night on the temple grounds, but the wording in this verse indicates she was wholly devoted to God.

Anna was quite public with her devotion as she "worshiped night and day, fasting and praying" (Luke 2:37), watching and waiting for the Messiah. She was incredibly devout. The presence of such Messiah-loving individuals creates a divergent picture of the temple atmosphere. Whereas religious sects were clinging together with their comrades to maneuver themselves into a position to rule the people and keep the Romans at bay, these devout and godly figures (Simeon and Anna) created excitement about God's intervention into the affairs of their nation.

Live It Out

A teenage mother gave birth to the Messiah. A young couple could never have imagined their role in a story that would change humanity forever. At the same time, people had waited for centuries for the Messiah to come. We can find ourselves in either of these situations—those who have been looking for meaning in their lives (Simeon and Anna) and those who find themselves suddenly and unexpectedly in the middle of God's story (Mary and Joseph). Where do you find yourself today?

God fulfilled his promise in Jesus. He keeps his word. His timing was perfect. Simeon was in the right place at the right time, long before the young couple came to the temple. Long before an angel had visited a young teenage girl, the Lord had raised up a prophetess by the name of Anna. Are you holding onto God's promises today? Are you seeking his comfort like Simeon? How have you responded to Jesus' arrival?

Questions

1. Why would Luke mention both Simeon and Anna?

2. How did Simeon recognize Jesus as the awaited Messiah?

3. To whom might Anna have spoken about Jesus?

4. How long are you willing to wait for God's promises to become a reality in your life?

5. Can you identify with the lives of Simeon or Anna? If so, how and why?

6. How does this passage change your perspective about Christmas and Advent?

ALL THE BIBLE FOR ALL OF LIFE

Our Next New Study

(Available for use beginning March 2016)

Choices and Consequences
(JOSHUA/JUDGES)

HOW TO ORDER
More Bible Study Materials

It's easy! Just fill in the following information. For additional Bible study materials available both in print and digital versions, see www.baptistwaypress.org, or get a complete order form by calling 1-866-249-1799 or e-mailing baptistway@texasbaptists.org.

Title of item	Price	Quantity	Cost
This Issue			
Jesus: King or Concierge? (Matthew)—Study Guide (BWP001207)	$4.25	_____	_____
Jesus: King or Concierge? (Matthew)—Large Print Study Guide (BWP001208)	$4.50	_____	_____
Jesus: King or Concierge? (Matthew)—Teaching Guide (BWP001209)	$4.95	_____	_____
Additional Issues Available			
Created for Relationships—Study Guide (BWP001197)	$3.95	_____	_____
Created for Relationships—Large Print Study Guide (BWP001198)	$4.25	_____	_____
Created for Relationships—Teaching Guide (BWP001199)	$4.95	_____	_____
14 Habits of Highly Effective Disciples—Study Guide (BWP001177)	$3.95	_____	_____
14 Habits of Highly Effective Disciples—Large Print Study Guide (BWP001178)	$4.25	_____	_____
14 Habits of Highly Effective Disciples—Teaching Guide (BWP001179)	$4.95	_____	_____
Guidance for the Seasons of Life—Study Guide (BWP001157)	$3.95	_____	_____
Guidance for the Seasons of Life—Large Print Study Guide (BWP001158)	$4.25	_____	_____
Guidance for the Seasons of Life—Teaching Guide (BWP001159)	$4.95	_____	_____
Living Generously for Jesus' Sake—Study Guide (BWP001137)	$3.95	_____	_____
Living Generously for Jesus' Sake—Large Print Study Guide (BWP001138)	$4.25	_____	_____
Living Generously for Jesus' Sake—Teaching Guide (BWP001139)	$4.95	_____	_____
Old Testament			
Exodus: Liberated for Life in Covenant with God—Study Guide (BWP001192)	$3.95	_____	_____
Exodus: Liberated for Life in Covenant with God—Large Print Study Guide (BWP001193)	$4.25	_____	_____
Exodus: Liberated for Life in Covenant with God—Teaching Guide (BWP001194)	$4.95	_____	_____
Psalms: Songs from the Heart of Faith—Study Guide (BWP001152)	$3.95	_____	_____
Psalms: Songs from the Heart of Faith—Large Print Study Guide (BWP001153)	$4.25	_____	_____
Psalms: Songs from the Heart of Faith—Teaching Guide (BWP001154)	$4.95	_____	_____
Jeremiah and Ezekiel: Prophets of Judgment and Hope—Study Guide (BWP001172)	$3.95	_____	_____
Jeremiah and Ezekiel: Prophets of Judgment and Hope—Large Print Study Guide (BWP001173)	$4.25	_____	_____
Jeremiah and Ezekiel: Prophets of Judgment and Hope—Teaching Guide (BWP001174)	$4.95	_____	_____
New Testament			
The Gospel of Mark: People Responding to Jesus—Study Guide (BWP001147)	$3.95	_____	_____
The Gospel of Mark: People Responding to Jesus—Large Print Study Guide (BWP001148)	$4.25	_____	_____
The Gospel of Mark: People Responding to Jesus—Teaching Guide (BWP001149)	$4.95	_____	_____
The Gospel of Luke: Jesus' Personal Touch—Study Guide (BWP001167)	$3.95	_____	_____
The Gospel of Luke: Jesus' Personal Touch—Large Print Study Guide (BWP001168)	$4.25	_____	_____
The Gospel of Luke: Jesus' Personal Touch—Teaching Guide (BWP001169)	$4.95	_____	_____
The Gospel of John: Believe in Jesus and Live!—Study Guide (BWP001187)	$3.95	_____	_____
The Gospel of John: Believe in Jesus and Live!—Large Print Study Guide (BWP001188)	$4.25	_____	_____
The Gospel of John: Believe in Jesus and Live!—Teaching Guide (BWP001189)	$4.95	_____	_____

The Book of Acts: Time to Act on Acts 1:8—Study Guide (BWP001142)	$3.95	_____	_____
The Book of Acts: Time to Act on Acts 1:8—Large Print Study Guide (BWP001143)	$4.25	_____	_____
The Book of Acts: Time to Act on Acts 1:8—Teaching Guide (BWP001144)	$4.95	_____	_____
Romans: A Gospel-Centered Worldview—Study Guide (BWP001202)	$4.25	_____	_____
Romans: A Gospel-Centered Worldview—Large Print Study Guide (BWP001203)	$4.50	_____	_____
Romans: A Gospel-Centered Worldview—Teaching Guide (BWP001204)	$4.95	_____	_____
Letters to the Ephesians and Timothy—Study Guide (BWP001182)	$3.95	_____	_____
Letters to the Ephesians and Timothy—Large Print Study Guide (BWP001183)	$4.25	_____	_____
Letters to the Ephesians and Timothy—Teaching Guide (BWP001184)	$4.95	_____	_____
Hebrews and the Letters of Peter—Study Guide (BWP001162)	$3.95	_____	_____
Hebrews and the Letters of Peter—Large Print Study Guide (BWP001163)	$4.25	_____	_____
Hebrews and the Letters of Peter—Teaching Guide (BWP001164)	$4.95	_____	_____

Coming for use beginning March 2016

Choices and Consequences (Joshua/Judges)—Study Guide (BWP001212)	$4.25	_____	_____
Choices and Consequences (Joshua/Judges)—Large Print Study Guide (BWP001213)	$4.50	_____	_____
Choices and Consequences (Joshua/Judges)—Teaching Guide (BWP001214)	$4.95	_____	_____

Cost of items (Order value) _____

Standard (UPS/Mail) Shipping Charges*			
Order Value	Shipping charge**	Order Value	Shipping charge**
$.01–$9.99	$6.50	$160.00–$199.99	$24.00
$10.00–$19.99	$8.50	$200.00–$249.99	$28.00
$20.00–$39.99	$9.50	$250.00–$299.99	$30.00
$40.00–$59.99	$10.50	$300.00–$349.99	$34.00
$60.00–$79.99	$11.50	$350.00–$399.99	$42.00
$80.00–$99.99	$12.50	$400.00–$499.99	$50.00
$100.00–$129.99	$15.00	$500.00–$599.99	$60.00
$130.00–$159.99	$20.00	$600.00–$799.99	$72.00**

Shipping charges (see chart*) _____

TOTAL _____

*Please call 1-866-249-1799 if the exact amount is needed prior to ordering.

**For order values $800.00 and above, please call 1-866-249-1799 or check www.baptistwaypress.org

Please allow two weeks for standard delivery.
For express shipping service: Call 1-866-249-1799 for information on additional charges.

YOUR NAME _____ PHONE _____

YOUR CHURCH _____ DATE ORDERED _____

SHIPPING ADDRESS _____

CITY _____ STATE _____ ZIP CODE _____

E-MAIL _____

MAIL this form with your check for the total amount to:
BAPTISTWAY PRESS, Baptist General Convention of Texas,
7557 Rambler Road, Suite 1200, Dallas, TX 75231–2388
(Make checks to "BaptistWay Press")

OR, **CALL** your order toll-free: 1-866-249-1799
(M-Fri 8:30 a.m.-5:00 p.m. central time).

OR, **E-MAIL** your order to: baptistway@texasbaptists.org.

OR, **ORDER ONLINE** at www.baptistwaypress.org.

We look forward to receiving your order! Thank you!